No
Ordinary
Book

Charles H. H. Scobie

No Ordinary Book

The Making and Meaning of the New Testament

Foreword by Gertrude McLaughlin, SNJM

NOVALIS

To my wife, Jean

Biblical quotations are from the *Revised Standard Version.*
Cover and design: Denis De Carufel

Novalis
P.O. Box 9700, Terminal
Ottawa, Ontario K1G 4B4

Wood Lake Books
P. O. Box 700
Winfield, British Columbia VOH 2CO

ISBN:
Novalis 2-89088-311-6
Wood Lake Books 919599-65-6

Printed in Canada

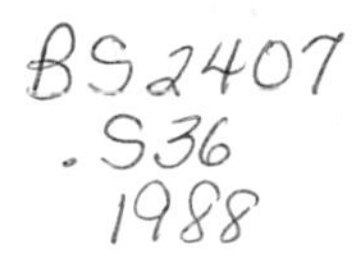

Contents

(Table A)

The Books of the New Testament in Their Canonical Order

Book	Abbreviation
The Gospel According to Matthew	Matt
The Gospel According to Mark	Mark
The Gospel According to Luke	Luke
The Gospel According to John	John
The Acts of the Apostles	Acts
The Letter of Paul to the Romans	Rom
The First Letter of Paul to the Corinthians	I Cor
The Second Letter of Paul to the Corinthians	II Cor
The Letter of Paul to the Galatians	Gal
The Letter of Paul to the Ephesians	Eph
The Letter of Paul to the Philippians	Phil
The Letter of Paul to the Colossians	Col
The First Letter of Paul to the Thessalonians	I Thess
The Second Letter of Paul to the Thessalonians	II Thess
The First Letter of Paul to Timothy	I Tim
The Second Letter of Paul to Timothy	II Tim
The Letter of Paul to Titus	Titus
The Letter of Paul to Philemon	Philem
The Letter to the Hebrews	Heb
The Letter of James	Jas
The First Letter of Peter	I Pet
The Second Letter of Peter	II Pet
The First Letter of John	I John
The Second Letter of John	II John
The Third Letter of John	III John
The Letter of Jude	Jude
The Revelation to John	Rev

(Table B)

The Books of the New Testament in Their Probable Chronological Order

8-4 B.C.?	Birth of Jesus
A.D. 30/33?	Crucifixion of Jesus Conversion of Paul
50	Paul in Corinth I, II THESSALONIANS I, II CORINTHIANS GALATIANS (considered by some to be Paul's earliest letter) ROMANS
60?	Paul's arrival in Rome PHILIPPIANS (placed by some in the mid-50s) COLOSSIANS PHILEMON EPHESIANS (if by Paul) I PETER (if by Peter)
64	Persecution of Christians in Rome under Nero Death of Peter and Paul
66	Outbreak of Jewish Revolt MARK
70	Fall of Jerusalem to the Romans HEBREWS JAMES MATTHEW LUKE-ACTS
95	Persecution under Domitian REVELATION JOHN I, II, III JOHN I, II TIMOTHY (if not by Paul in their present form) TITUS (if not by Paul in its present form)
112	Persecution under Trajan JUDE II PETER (if not by Peter)
132-135	Second Jewish Revolt

Foreword

The joint publication of Dr. Charles Scobie's book by Novalis and Wood Lake Books marks another milestone in the growing collaboration between Catholics and Protestants in the study of the Bible. Once a cause of controversy and division, Bible study is now the source of our mutual respect and understanding. By returning to our roots in the written Word of God, we are discovering how much we have in common.

Not so very long ago it was unthinkable that a Lutheran would be president of the Catholic Biblical Association or that a Catholic priest would be president of the Society for New Testament Studies, but that's in fact the case today.

This is not the only level at which Catholics and Protestants are working together. Most translation projects undertaken by the United Bible Societies have members from several faiths on their teams. The second Vatican Council encouraged Catholic participation in such endeavours, with a view to producing Bibles that "all Christians will be able to use." Tangible results are evident here in Canada where Québec schools have adopted the Good News Bible *and* La Bible en français courant *as the texts for religious instruction. Both are produced by the Canadian Bible Society, which was once considered a bastion of very sectarian Protestantism!*

In every community and congregation today there is growing interest in Bible study. Instead of praying and studying it alone, people are joining groups to share their insights into the Word of God, as well as their love and understanding of it. And for groups such as these, Dr. Scobie's book is a treasure. He has brought the latest and surest findings in biblical research to the level of the interested person who is without preparation in the area of New Testament studies.

From beginning to end, the love and learning of a skilled teacher are evident in No Ordinary Book. *To clarify a point he uses apt examples either from Scripture itself or from everyday life. He makes the text come alive as he applies it to the twentieth century. His introduction to the letters to the Corinthians (p. 75), for instance, proves how things have changed very little in the last two thousand years. But he stresses that "we must first understand what the New Testament writers were saying to the Christians of their own era before we can go on to discover what they have to say to Christians today." This is a principle to which he is true throughout the book.*

An interesting aspect of No Ordinary Book *is the space devoted to the making of the New Testament. Much is written about its meaning, but there is precious little at the popular level on how it came into being in the first century and on how it has come across the ages to reach us. Dr. Scobie's description of modern methods and tools of research is especially useful for the ordinary reader puzzled by the many forms of biblical criticism used today in the study of the Bible.*

Above all, No Ordinary Book *is a testimony to the love and faith of a scholar who has spent his life studying and teaching God's Word. This is the true ecumenical dimension of Dr. Scobie's work. For this we thank him.*

Gertrude McLaughlin, SNJM
Vice President (1984-87)
Canadian Bible Society

Preface

This book has been many years in the making. It reflects my conviction that scholars should not remain in their academic cloisters, that they have an obligation to communicate the results of scholarship to the general public. Biblical scholars in particular have a duty to pass on and interpret their findings to the men and women of the Church. I have frequently sought to do this through both the written and spoken word, and this volume in many ways sums up my attempts in this regard over the years.

Chapters 6 through 20 are based on my series of articles on "The Making and Meaning of the New Testament" which appeared in the Presbyterian Record *between 1979 and 1982. I am grateful to the editor, the Rev. James Ross Dickey, whom I am proud to count as one of my former students, for his encouragement and assistance in the publication of the articles, as well as for his suggestion that they be revised, expanded and published in book form.*

I wish to thank Ralph Milton of Wood Lake Books for his reactions to the first draft of this work and for his helpful suggestions. Special thanks are due to editor Michael O'Hearn of Novalis for seeing the book through the process of publication, and for providing both correction and guidance in such a tactful and helpful way. I am grateful also to my secretary Robin Hamilton for assistance with word-processing and for entering corrections and revisions with such care.

Direct references to books or articles are acknowledged in footnotes; however, these have been relegated to the end of the book since there is no need to consult them while reading the text. Those of you familiar with the field of New Testament study will recognize the great debt I owe to many scholars and writers, far too numerous for me to acknowledge here.

Charles H. H. Scobie
Department of Religious Studies
Mount Allison University
January 1988

Introduction

This book is written from two convictions. The first is that the New Testament is no ordinary book. For the best part of two thousand years believing Christians have found in it not only the words of human authors but also the Word of God, speaking to their situation, challenging and provoking them, guiding and comforting them. The second conviction is that the New Testament should be read and studied intelligently, with all the help that modern discoveries and modern scholarship can provide.

There is, of course, no substitute for reading and studying the New Testament itself. This book will fail unless it encourages you to do so. Since the New Testament is not the easiest book to understand, this volume seeks to give you some basic information on its making and meaning and to provide some basic guidance on how best to read and study it.

A vast number of books about the New Testament have been produced over the past fifty years, but many of these are not suitable for the general reader, making frequent use of technical theological terms and often requiring at least some knowledge of Greek. My aim in writing this book has been to use language that is as clear and non-technical as possible.

No prior knowledge of the subject on the part of the reader is assumed. On the other hand the book does presuppose and is deeply indebted to contemporary New Testament scholarship even when this is explicitly referred to only in passing.

My hope is that this book will be of interest and help to a wide circle of readers. Though written primarily for members of the Christian Church who want to understand better the basis of their faith, it is also addressed to those who are interested in Christianity, whether or not they are at present committed to it, and even to those who are merely curious about the foundation document of the Christian faith.

I hope that Christians of all denominations and shades of theological opinion will find this book useful. One of the exciting trends of recent years has been the emphasis in the Roman Catholic Church that all believers read and study the Bible in their own language. Protestant and Roman Catholic scholars today co-operate in all aspects of biblical scholarship. In fact, there are many contemporary examples of books and commentaries being published where it is difficult to tell to what branch of the Christian Church the author belongs. This is not to say that there are no differences of opinion on the meaning and interpretation of the New Testament, but these differences increasingly tend to cut across denominational lines.

Unfortunately there appears to be a growing polarization between "liberals" and "conservatives" in the interpretation of Scripture. Those who may be labelled "conservative" tend to take the whole of the Bible as literally true, cannot contemplate differences or errors of any kind in God's word, stress the unity of Scripture and interpret it in conformity with orthodox Christian doctrine as laid down in the classic creeds and confessions of the Christian Church. Those who may be labelled "liberal" do not take the whole of the Bible literally, believe that we have the treasure of God's word in earthen vessels and so can accept that there may be differences and even discrepancies within the Bible, and feel that many traditional doctrines need to be reinterpreted in the late twentieth century. There are a great many Christians, however, who fit neither of these descriptions; they find themselves somewhere in between the two extremes.

This book does not promote any particular theological point of view. With so-called "liberals" I agree that we must listen to what modern biblical scholars have to say and follow the historical and critical approach, even when it may upset our hallowed traditions and preconceived notions. But with so-called "conservatives" I do not believe that the New Testament should be approached only on a human level; it is also the means by which God continues to speak to his people, the Church, in the present day. While it certainly contains a wide variety of emphases, it has also a basic unity of thought and purpose. Some liberals may find this book too conservative and some conservatives may find it too liberal. I hope that many will find the approach adopted here both sane and helpful and that it will prove valuable to the committed believer and to the interested enquirer.

When reading this book you should have a copy of the New Testament, preferably in a reliable modern translation (for information on translations see chapter 5). The arrangement of the different books in the New Testament is known as the "canonical" order, that is, the order in which they came to be placed in the "canon" or authorized list of books regarded as constituting sacred Scripture. The list is given in Table A — The Books of the New Testament in Their Canonical Order (page 7).

Unfortunately the canonical order is not the order in which the books were written. However, careful study of the New Testament has enabled scholars to arrange them at least roughly in the order of writing. See Table B — The Books of the New Testament in Their Probable Chronological Order (page 8). It must be noted that the dating of the books is at best approximate. Moreover, not all scholars are agreed on the dating in every case.

In Part II of this book an introduction is provided to each of the books of the New Testament. In the main, the probable chronological order has been followed although, in one or two cases, groups of books have been discussed because they logically go together. Readers may wish to refer to Table B from time to time to be reminded of how each book fits in to the historical development of the early Christian Church.

For those who wish to use this book in a Bible study or discussion group, a separate study guide is available from the publisher. It includes a section on "Books on the New Testament" with suggestions for further study.

PART I
INTRODUCING THE NEW TESTAMENT

1. The Nature of the New Testament

By any reckoning the New Testament is the most influential book ever written. Along with the Old Testament it forms the Bible, the sacred scriptures of Christianity, a faith which has had enormous influence over the past two thousand years, especially in the West, and which today claims far more adherents than any other world religion. Despite differences of interpretation the New Testament is the charter and constitution of the faith for Protestants, Catholics and Orthodox Christians alike and has a central place in determining their beliefs, worship and life style.

The New Testament has been translated into far more languages than any other book in human history. As Christianity continues to spread to new areas and new peoples the New Testament, or portions of it, is generally translated first; the whole Bible is a longer, more difficult and more costly work to produce. A recent count reveals that the New Testament has been translated into over 1600 languages, but that is a figure subject to constant upward revision.

A Book Set Apart

For Christians the New Testament is the most important part of "the Holy Bible." The word "holy" basically means "separate" or "set apart"; the Bible is a book which is different and special, set apart from all other books. For Christian believers it does not merely contain the words of human beings written many centuries ago; it is also the "word of God" which still addresses and challenges the people of God today. Another way of expressing this is to say that the New Testament is "inspired," the root meaning of which is that God "breathed into" or imparted his Spirit to the original authors.

Over the centuries learned theologians have come back again and again to the books of the New Testament as they have wrestled with the doctrines of the Christian faith and have sought to appropriate them and apply them in new situations and changing circumstances. As well, countless ordinary Christian believers have turned to the New Testament to seek God's guidance and help in their daily lives. The millions of copies of the New Testament in modern translations which have been sold in recent years show that people, more than ever, are eager to read and study this book for themselves.

Yet the New Testament is not the easiest book to read and understand, and even when we make a conscientious effort it can seem remote from the world in which we live. We read of a Galilean teacher who lived nearly two thousand years ago, or we read letters giving advice to little groups of Christians in towns and cities of the Roman Empire. What relevance does this have today to people living in a world of jet-planes and space travel, of television and computers, a world so different from that into which Jesus was born?

How does the New Testament become the word of God for Christians today? The process is certainly not a magical one — as in the case of the woman who believed in simply letting her Bible fall open at any page, putting her finger on a verse and assuming that it gave God's message to her. One day she did this and came up with the verse, "Judas went and hanged himself." Deciding to give God a second chance she tried again and this time got, "Go and do thou likewise!"

While there are certain well-loved passages to which people may turn again and again and which they can read without introduction or comment, generally speaking some knowledge of the *making* of the New Testament is essential and extremely helpful as we seek to discover its *meaning*. One does not have to be a scholar to read and understand the New Testament, but everyone can benefit from the work that scholars have done and continue to do. It is helpful at the outset to recognize some of the main ways in which scholars have approached the New Testament.

The Traditional Approach

Most modern books begin with a title page giving the title of the book, the name of the author, and often the publisher and date as well. A preface tells us how and why the book was written, while the book jacket gives us a short biography and perhaps even a photograph of the author. But we get nothing like this in the books of the New Testament. It surprises many people to discover that all four Gospels were originally anonymous works! The titles which are familiar to us, "According to Matthew," "According to Mark," and so on, were added later when the four Gospels were collected together. In the text of the Gospels themselves, however, no author is ever named. Modern authors (especially professors!) want to take all the credit they can get for writing a book, but the Gospel writers were content to remain anonymous. They had no thought of drawing attention to themselves: their one aim was to direct their readers' attention to Christ. Even where authors' names are given (Paul, Peter, James, Jude, John) there is generally a minimum of information concerning where, when, how and why the books were written.

A number of Christian writers from the early centuries do pass on "traditions" concerning the writing of the books of the New Testament, but this information tends to be scrappy and not necessarily reliable. It is not always clear to what extent these traditions are based on hard information and how much simply on inspired guesswork.

After the first few centuries the Church developed what we may call "the traditional approach." Set answers were provided to all the standard questions. Which Gospel was the first to be written? Answer: Matthew. Who wrote the Fourth Gospel, the Letters of John and the Book of Revelation? Answer: The Apostle John wrote all five. There was a strong tendency to attribute books wherever possible to one of the apostles, that special group of individuals chosen and sent out by Jesus as preachers and leaders of the Church. By and large these traditional answers came to be accepted without question.

The Historical Approach

For many centuries Christians were content to accept the traditional answers which were handed out to them on a plate. Around the late eighteenth and early nineteenth centuries, however, a new method of studying the Bible began to emerge. It generally became known as "the historical approach." It basically recognizes that the New Testament did not drop from heaven ready-made. The twenty-seven books were written by various authors over a period of perhaps seventy or eighty years. They were written within early Christian communities, in the first instance to meet quite specific needs and situations. Hence the New Testament cannot really be understood other than in the context of the life and work of the early Church. This method is therefore historical in that it tries to place the books in their original setting in the history of the early Church.

This is also referred to as the "critical" approach. It is critical, not in the negative sense of trying to find fault, but in the positive sense of examining the evidence rather than simply being content with traditional answers, and of attempting to sift fact from fiction, the true from the false. This approach, originally developed mainly by Protestant scholars, has revolutionized our understanding of the New Testament. Many Christians initially viewed it with suspicion and, indeed, some still do today. It has challenged some of the "traditional" views, for example, on the authorship of books of the New Testament or on their date of writing. While it is true that some scholars who adopted this approach have reached seemingly unduly sceptical conclusions, this does not have to be the case. In any event, Christians must surely be committed to seeking the truth even when the search overturns some long-held and cherished notions. In recent years the Roman Catholic church has joined the majority of Protestants in accepting this approach. Today it is rejected only by more extreme conservative Protestants who still defend the traditional views (though Protestants are supposed to support the evidence of Scripture itself in preference to Church tradition!).

The historical approach recognizes that the New Testament has to be seen against its true historical background. Jesus and his disciples were all Jews, and for the *religious* background of the New Testament the Hebrew Scriptures are naturally of prime importance. Judaism underwent some important developments in the first and second centuries B.C. and the first century A.D., and New Testament scholars also recognize the importance of studying the religious works produced in this period, especially the writings of the Jewish philosopher Philo (c. 20 B.C. — A.D. 50) and the Jewish historian Josephus (c. A.D. 37 — 100), as well as the teachings of the Rabbis later codified in the Mishnah and Talmud.

Christianity spread outwards from Palestine against a *cultural* background which was still profoundly Greek. The most obvious indication of this is the fact that the common language of the time was Greek. Although Jesus' native tongue was Aramaic, all the books of the New Testament were written in what scholars call Hellenistic or *Koine* (i.e. "common") Greek. Greek philosophy and religion still exerted a strong influence, and early Christian leaders such as Paul had to express their Christian faith in terms understandable to those whose cultural background was basically Greek.

The mighty Roman Empire constituted the *political* background of the New Testament. Palestine had been taken over by Rome in the first century B.C. and was ruled at first by a puppet king, Herod the Great, then more directly by Roman officials such as Pontius Pilate, the procurator or prefect of Judaea who had Jesus put to death. Christianity spread through various provinces of the Empire, reaching the capital Rome at an early stage. From the later books of the New Testament it is already apparent that the early Church was on a collision course with the Roman political authorities.

Against this background, New Testament scholars seek to trace the origins and development of the Christian Church out of which the books of the New Testament emerged. They can benefit from the vast amount of work which has been done by historians of the ancient world. Archaeological discoveries continue to provide an exciting source of new data. Recent examples include the Bodmer Papyri (early manuscripts of the New Testament itself), the famous Dead Sea Scrolls from shortly before New Testament times, and the less well-known Nag Hammadi codices from the early Christian centuries, all of which have come to light since the Second World War. More recently biblical scholars have been turning to the social sciences for help in understanding the way in which the early Church saw itself and its relation to the surrounding society and culture. Even when little is known about the author of a New Testament book, we can develop a "profile" of the community from which it emerged that will enhance our understanding of the book.

The historical approach does not deny that the books of the New Testament are of lasting value and are capable of speaking to Christians today, but it does maintain that we must first understand what the New Testament writers were saying to the Christians of their own era before we can go on to discover what they have to say to Christians today.

The Literary Approach

The New Testament is not only a volume for devotional reading and a source for the history of the early Church; it is also a body of literature. It is, in fact, a small library consisting of twenty-seven separate literary works.

While this insight is certainly not new, recent years have seen a greatly increased interest in what may be called "the literary approach." This view is not as concerned with the historical background and origin of a work as it is with the work itself in its completed form. Once a book is written, copied out and circulated, it assumes a life of its own, and it constitutes its own world of meaning. One can thus study and appreciate it as a work of literature in its own right.

The identification of different types of literature is basic. Thus in the New Testament we have four *Gospels,* a new and distinct type of literature, which proclaims the Good News through an account of Jesus' ministry and especially of his death and resurrection. There is one *history,* the Book of Acts, which stands in the tradition both of the historical books of the Old Testament and of Greek historical writing. There are a number of *letters* which to varying degrees follow the generally accepted pattern of letters in the ancient world. Finally, there is an *apocalypse,* a type of literature strange to us but well-known to many Jewish readers of the period. The word "apocalypse" means literally an "uncovering," that is, a making known or a revelation of something previously hidden. It is used particularly to refer to those Jewish books which claimed to reveal truths concerning the struggle between good and evil climaxing in the final defeat of evil and the ushering in of God's Kingdom.

The literary approach is concerned with language and style. For example, it is important to recognize that there are passages of poetry in the New Testament. Identification of various figures of speech, of themes and motifs, of imagery and symbolism all aid in the understanding of the literature of the New Testament.

This approach uses a variety of methods, some well-established and traditional, others new and experimental. Some scholars today, for example, are working on what is known as "rhetorical criticism." Rhetoric, "the art of persuasive speech," was highly developed in ancient times and New Testament writers employed rhetorical techniques which were widely known. A knowledge of these techniques helps us understand and appreciate how the authors of the New Testament sought to appeal to and convince their readers by what they wrote and by the way they wrote it. Another more advanced method which has been applied to the New Testament is known as "structuralism"; drawing on developments in anthropology as well as literature, it seeks to penetrate to the "deep structures" underlying the text which manifest aspects of human existence and human experience which are the same for peoples of all times and places.

This approach is neutral as far as Christian belief is concerned. A non-Christian can certainly appreciate the New Testament from a purely literary point of view. Nevertheless there is much in this approach which is of value to Christian believers and which can assist their understanding and appreciation of the New Testament as the word of God.

Rich Diversity but Basic Unity

One benefit of both the historical and literary approaches to the New Testament has been to disclose the rich diversity of its contents. Mark and Luke, along with Paul and John, were not just shorthand typists taking down a divinely dictated message. They were real flesh and blood people with different characters, temperaments and outlooks whose Christian experience and whose apprehension of the Truth varied considerably from one to the other. To be sure, these differences can be exaggerated and some recent scholarship has tended to overemphasize the differences among them. Behind all the variety there is a basic unity, a common belief in the "Gospel" or "Good News" of what God has done for us in Jesus Christ and in the type of response which Christians are called upon to make.

2. The Cornerstone of the New Testament

Without Jesus there would be no New Testament: it is a simple as that. More than one New Testament writer pictures Jesus as the "cornerstone" (see Eph 2:20, I Pet 2:6) and, certainly, as far as the New Testament itself is concerned, Jesus *is* the cornerstone; take that way and the whole structure would collapse.

We have to remember, however, that Jesus did not write any part of the New Testament; he left no written record of any kind. Moreover there were no television cameras or cassette tape-recorders to preserve what he looked like or what he said. The fact is that we have no *direct* access to the Jesus of history at all.

A few brief references to Jesus are found in the Jewish historian Josephus and the early second century Roman historians Tacitus and Suetonius, but they give nothing that we do not already know from the Gospels. Jewish sources (Talmud) make occasional hostile references to Jesus but they provide a minimum of information.[1] Various "apocryphal" gospels circulated in the early Church, filling out details of the life of Jesus and especially of his infancy, but it is generally agreed that they are largely works of fiction. The letters of the New Testament written by Paul and others surprisingly make almost no reference to any details of Jesus' earthly life. For our knowledge of Jesus we are thus almost entirely dependent on the four Gospels traditionally ascribed to Matthew, Mark, Luke and John.

The task seems simple then: all we have to do is read the four Gospels and we will know exactly what kind of person this Jesus was and what he stood for. Unfortunately, experience suggests that the matter is not quite as simple as this. On the basis of the Gospels the most diverse interpretations of Jesus have been put forward. During the nineteenth century anybody who was anybody had to write a "Life of Jesus." In a famous book written in the early years of this century, *The Quest of the Historical Jesus,* Albert Schweitzer surveyed these "Lives" and showed how easily each author had come up with the Jesus he was looking for, the Jesus who fitted the writer's own outlook and presuppositions.[2] During the Second World War there were those who thought Christianity could be reconciled with Hitler's philosophy through a form of "German Christianity," while in a country like Holland there were others whose interpretation of Jesus led them to risk their lives to help Jews escape from the Nazis. In our own day, a right-wing dictator may profess to believe in Jesus and may argue that Jesus taught the people always to obey the government, while a guerilla fighting for the overthrow of the regime may equally claim to follow Jesus and may cite him in support of a "theology of liberation."

The Writing of the Gospels

To understand how such divergent interpretations are possible we have to try to understand how the Gospels came to be written, a matter which has been the subject of intense study by scholars over the past two hundred or so years.

From the earliest times considerable differences were noted in the Gospels, especially between John, on the one hand, and Matthew, Mark, and Luke on the other. In the second century the Church found itself with three options. One was favoured by the heretic Marcion: he wanted to accept only *one* of the Gospels (in his case Luke) and reject the other three. A second possibility was represented by Tatian who combined all four Gospels into one work, his *Diatessaron* ("four-in-one"), a harmony which removed all differences among the Gospels. The third option and the one which the Church chose was argued by

Irenaeus: accept all four Gospels, despite their differences, recognizing that Christ "when he was manifest to mankind, gave us the Gospel under four forms but bound together by the one Spirit."[3]

Over the centuries various attempts were made to reconcile the differences, but it is only in modern times that scholars have come up with a satisfactory explanation of both the resemblances and the differences among the four Gospels.

Today it is generally accepted that the traditions of Jesus' words and deeds must have been passed on by word of mouth for at least a generation. *Form criticism* is the discipline which studies this period of "oral tradition." The greater part of the Gospels consists of fairly short, paragraphed-sized units which tend to conform to certain patterns or forms, thus making them easier to memorize. (Hence the name "form criticism.")

Like it or not, we are forced to admit that this part of the process was very selective. There is so much about Jesus that we would like to know but which was *not* remembered and passed on. What did Jesus look like? Was he tall or short, dark or fair? What kind of education did he receive? What happened to him as a child or as a teenager? There is truth in the view that we cannot write a "biography" of Jesus since so much of the kind of information a modern biographer needs simply is not there. Scholars stress that the material which did survive was selected because it served the needs of the early Christian communities, especially their preaching, teaching, controversy and worship.

At the next stage some material began to be written down in the form of short tracts or pamphlets. This is where *source criticism* comes into play. There are indications that behind our written Gospels lay earlier written sources, for example, short collections of the sayings of Jesus, as well as collections of Old Testament texts fulfilled in the life of Christ. A chapter such as Mark 13 may have begun life as a separate tract about the end time, while almost certainly the story of Jesus' passion must have been put together as a connected narrative at an early stage.

The overwhelming majority of scholars today agree that Mark's Gospel was the first to be written, though even he must have drawn upon a variety of these earlier sources. Both Matthew and Luke wrote later than Mark and used his Gospel as one of their sources. In addition, Matthew and Luke appear to have had in common some other collection of the sayings of Jesus which has not survived separately, but which is commonly designated as the "Q" source (from the German *Quelle*, meaning "source"). Matthew and Luke also had still further sources, whether oral or written. This helps explain the material peculiar to Matthew (for example, the story of the Wise Men), and the material peculiar to Luke (for example, the parable of the Good Samaritan). John probably wrote independently of the other three (though this is a matter of debate) and drew on his own sources. This is the modern view of the composition of the Gospels. Yet, if we read the introduction to Luke's Gospel (1:1-4) we see that it actually corresponds very closely with what one Gospel writer at least tells us: he was not himself an eyewitness of the life of Christ, but he spent some time gathering as many reliable sources as he could and then rearranging this material into a readable and informative account.

This suggests the writers of the Gospels are more editors and compilers than original authors. This stage of the process is studied by *redaction criticism,* "redaction" being an alternate term for "editing." All the Gospel writers used earlier materials — oral and/or written — and wrote up the story in somewhat the same way as newspaper sub-editors write up a feature based on material sent in by reporters.

At one time the Gospel writers were regarded simply as scissors-and-paste compilers of scrapbooks on the life of Jesus. Redaction Criticism has radically changed that view. Any historian or biographer is an interpreter who writes from a certain point of view. By what they choose to include or leave out, and by the way they arrange and present their material, all four Gospel writers show that they are *theologians.* Each has his own quite distinct and profound understanding of the Christian faith.

Redaction criticism seeks to distinguish traditional material (oral and written) from editorial passages, arguing that the viewpoint of the Gospel writers is most evident in the latter. This works reasonably well with Matthew and Luke since we have at least one of their sources (Mark) and can study how they used that source. The sources of Mark and John, however, are much more a matter of speculation. Thus, while this approach has proved useful, it also has certain limitations.

While form criticism, source criticism and redaction criticism have shed a great deal of light on the quite complex historical process by which the Gospels gradually came into being, they are all based on historical reconstruction which inevitably deals with possibilities and probabilities rather than with certainties. Moreover, they all tend to chop the Gospel up into pieces, seeking to distinguish oral tradition, written sources and editorial comment. What we can be sure of is the completed Gospels as they have come down to us and this is where *literary criticism* is a helpful corrective.

This approach insists on viewing each Gospel as a whole. Even those who are reasonably familiar with the Gospels tend to read them in snippets or hear extracts read in church. One of the best things to do is to read right through the Gospels from beginning to end (try starting with Mark which is the shortest one). This will help you better appreciate the literary style and structure of each Gospel, and more easily recognize the picture of Christ which they present.

Facts Plus Interpretation

A very important contribution of modern scholarship is the recognition that the Gospels contain not just "mere facts," but facts plus interpretation.

Early Christians collected passages from the Old Testament and linked them with events in Jesus' life. In this way they brought out another dimension of the Christ event. The ministry of Jesus, they were saying, marks the breaking in of the new age foretold in the Old Testament. Under the guidance of the Holy Spirit early Christian preachers and teachers and the Gospel writers themselves discovered deeper and deeper levels of truth in the Gospel accounts, truth which either was missed or barely noticed when the events themselves were taking place prior to Jesus' resurrection and the giving of the Holy Spirit to the Church. Those who think that this is some kind of "modernistic" theory should reflect on how often the Gospels themselves comment on the disciples' slowness to learn and understand what was going on. There is so much that became clear only later on, looking back on events. John's Gospel recounts the story of Jesus' cleansing of the Temple (John 2:13-22). It brings out the significance of that event partly by linking it with certain Old Testament passages and partly by explaining the meaning of what Jesus did. But it is quite open in recognizing that it was only when "he was raised from the dead" that "his disciples remembered that he had said this; and they believed the scripture and the word which Jesus had spoken" (John 2:22).

The Gospels thus provide not just one, but four interpretations of Christ, and this has always bothered some people. The Gospels have often been referred to as portraits of Jesus and perhaps this is a helpful way of thinking of them. A painted portrait is not the same as a photograph. To examine a portrait under a magnifying glass, looking for photographic realism, will miss the point. That is because a good portrait can convey truths about a person's character and personality which a photograph cannot. Further, four portraits can tell us more than one and can supplement and correct each other.

This is not to deny that the Gospels go back ultimately to memories of the words and deeds of Jesus. At the same time, however, it is not always easy to sort out historical tradition from later interpretation. We need not follow the lead of some scholars who have carried scepticism to the extreme and suggested that we can know almost nothing about the historical Jesus other than that he existed. Much recent scholarship has moved cautiously back to affirming that there is a basic core of material on the historical Jesus which can be accepted as authentic.

For example, it has been demonstrated that in some of the recorded sayings of Jesus the original Aramaic language he spoke shows through the Greek of the Gospels. There are many passages which reflect an accurate knowledge of the Palestinian background of Jesus' ministry. Many of Jesus' sayings (like those of the Old Testament prophets) are in poetry, a fact suggesting Jesus gave them to his disciples in that form so they could more easily memorize them and pass them on to others. Where a feature of Jesus' ministry has "multiple attestation," that is, appears in several Gospels or in several sources, both earlier and later, it is difficult to deny that it goes back to the historical Jesus. In recent years some scholars have also appealed to what is called "the criterion of dissimilarity." Even if we prefer to err on the safe side we are forced to recognize elements which are quite distinctive and, indeed, unique in the life and teaching of Jesus. The Jesus of the Gospels differs from his Jewish background and also in some ways from Paul and later Christian writers. After all their studies, therefore, many scholars still find in the Gospels the record of a unique personality who continues to reach from the pages and challenge the reader to "follow me."

The Life and Teaching of Jesus

Keeping in mind, then, the danger of creating a distorted picture, we may, nevertheless, attempt to give a brief sketch of the life and teaching of Jesus.

Jesus began his public career by identifying himself with John the Baptist and his movement. After lying dormant for centuries the spirit of Old Testament prophecy came back to life in John's preaching. Believing that the great crisis of human history was almost at hand, John appealed to God's people to prepare for the end.

While John proclaimed that the crisis was near, Jesus went beyond this and proclaimed that the crisis was already here and had already begun. All present day scholars agree that the centre of Jesus' message was his proclamation of the Kingdom of God. Mark 1:15 provides a good summary: "The time is fulfilled, the Kingdom of God is at hand; repent, and believe in the gospel." This breaking into history of the rule or reign of God is closely tied to the person of Jesus himself. In him the hopes and longings of the Old Testament for the coming of a new age and a new order find their fulfilment: "Blessed are the eyes which see what you see! For I tell you that many prophets and kings desired to see what you see, and did not see it, and to hear what you hear, and did not hear it" (Luke 10:23, 24).

There is no doubt that Jesus believed in a *future* Day of Judgment and in the final triumph of God's Kingdom. He taught his disciples to pray for the coming of the Kingdom (Luke 11:2) and vividly portrayed the Judgment, for example, in the parable of the Sheep and the Goats (Matt 25:31-46). But the most striking thing about Jesus' message was his proclamation that the Kingdom of God is already *present:* "But if it is by the finger (or the Spirit) of God that I cast our demons, then the Kingdom of God has come upon you" (Luke 11:20, Matt 12:28). As Jesus preaches and teaches, heals the sick and reaches out to the outcasts, the Kingdom is already at work — for those who have eyes to see it!

It is clear that Jesus' conception of the Kingdom was very different from that of most of his contemporaries. Despite some recent claims to the contrary, Jesus had no sympathy for those who looked for nationalistic and violent solutions, who wanted to start a rebellion and drive the hated Romans into the sea. Equally, Jesus gave no encouragement to those who hoped that God would save the situation immediately by a dramatic supernatural intervention! He discouraged those who tried to forecast the time of the end: "The Kingdom of God is not coming with signs to be observed; nor will they say, 'Lo, here it is!' or 'There!' for behold, the Kingdom of God is in the midst of you" (Luke 17:20, 21). When he was arrested he refused to fight and, equally, he refused to call on God to send a legion of angels to his rescue (Matt 26:52, 53).

The breaking in of God's Kingdom challenges Jesus' hearers to a decision: do they enter the Kingdom or remain outside? To enter the Kingdom is worth any sacrifice, like a man who finds a treasure hidden in a field and sells all he has in order to gain it (Matt 13:44). Jesus' view of the Kingdom challenges conventional piety and wisdom and, in fact, reverses most people's accepted notions: in God's Kingdom, "Many that are first will be last, and the last first" (Mark 10:31). Again and again Jesus' parables bring out some startling aspect of the Kingdom.

Jesus summoned people to decision and, also, to discipleship. From a wider group of disciples he chose twelve, a number which immediately recalls the twelve tribes of Israel and suggests that Jesus chose them as the nucleus of the true Israel, a renewed people of God (Matt 19:28). With his disciples Jesus shared meals which anticipated the joy and fellowship of the heavenly banquet in God's Kingdom.

Everyone knows that Jesus summed up his ethical teaching by the commands to love God and to love one's neighbour (Mark 12:28-31), but not everyone realizes how extraordinarily demanding Jesus' teaching really is. A rude shock awaits those who would like to define carefully who their neighbour is (see the parable of the Good Samaritan, Luke 10:30-37). We are to love not just our friends but even our enemies (Matt 5:43, 44). Peter thought he was doing well if he forgave seven times in a row, but Jesus demanded "seventy times seven" which, in his arithmetic, meant an infinite number of times (Matt 18:21, 22). It is not just the outer act but the inner motive that must be pure (Matt 5:21-30, Mark 7:15). Of course, humanly speaking this is an impossible ideal, but "What is impossible with men is possible with God" (Luke 18:27). The Sermon on the Mount (Matt 5-7) is not a handbook of ethics for general consumption: it sketches the lifestyle of those who have responded to the grace and goodness of God and entered the Kingdom.

In Jesus' day many Jews looked for some type of "Messiah" which literally means "the anointed one," that is, the one chosen by God to usher in salvation; the Greek form of the same word is "Christos" or "Christ." Such expectations could take many forms depending on whether people looked for a new king or prophet or priest, and on whether they expected a more human or divine figure. The very essence of Christianity was to be the recognition of Jesus as the promised Messiah and the Son of God.

It is puzzling to many, therefore, to discover that some modern scholars have seriously questioned whether Jesus actually claimed these titles for himself in his own lifetime. Yet, when we study the Gospels carefully it does appear that Jesus was at least *reticent* in the claims he made for himself. A study of Mark (the earliest Gospel) in particular suggests that Jesus did not publicly claim the title "Messiah" during his ministry. There would, in fact, be a very good reason for this: the title would suggest to most people a kingly, political and military figure which is not at all what Jesus wanted to convey.

On the other hand, it is clear that Jesus stood in a unique relationship to God. He dared to address God as *Abba* (Mark 14:36), in Aramaic the familiar and family term for "Father." Almost the equivalent of "Daddy," it was never used in Jewish prayers to God. Moreover, he did speak frequently of the "Son of man" and directly or indirectly linked that title to himself. Deriving from Daniel 7 where it represents God's faithful people, "Son of man" does not just refer to the humanity of

Jesus: it is used to refer to an exalted, Messiah-like figure, but without political overtones.

If Jesus was reticent about making *explicit* claims, those *implicit* in his ministry were staggering. In his miracles it is the power of God which is at work, launching the attack against Satan and the powers of evil (Mark 3:22-27). Jesus dares to forgive people's sins, exercising an authority which in Jewish thought belonged to God alone (Mark 2:5-7). In reaching out to the outcasts of society Jesus not only proclaims the grace of God, he embodies it. For Jews God's supreme revelation had been given through Moses; Jesus dares to set aside provisions of the Law and declare the will of God directly (Mark 10:2-9).

Jesus thus made the most tremendous implicit claims, but he never hit people over the head and demanded that they had better believe it; rather, he challenged people to decide for themselves who he was. He even left John the Baptist to make up his own mind (Luke 7:18-23).

Jesus' brief ministry came to a climax with a last visit to Jerusalem where he went to launch a final appeal and challenge to God's people and, especially, to their leaders. But pressures were building up to silence the one who had done too much to upset the establishment and had challenged too many accepted ideas. Many people contributed to Jesus' death: the leaders of the Pharisees, offended by his teaching; the leaders of the priestly Sadducees whose privileges were threatened; Judas who betrayed his lord; the disciples who deserted him; Pilate who allowed himself to be blackmailed; the crowd, so easily swayed; the false witnesses who lied for money; and a squad of Roman soldiers who were simply obeying orders.

Jesus was executed by crucifixion, a cruel form of death reserved for common criminals. If that were the end of the story Jesus would have joined the ranks of martyred prophets and been relegated to the pages of history. That this did not happen is due to the event which launched the Christian movement — the resurrection of Jesus from the dead.

3.
The Setting of the New Testament

In order to understand the books of the New Testament we must try to see them in their original setting, that is, in the context of the developing life and work of the early Church. We must remember that Paul's letters, which are the earliest writings of the New Testament, date from twenty or more years after Jesus' death and, even then, most were hastily written to meet particular crisis situations. The first real Christian "book," the Gospel of Mark, dates from between thirty and forty years after the death of Jesus. The earliest Christians felt little need for written material: the apostles and others were available to tell of the words and deeds of Jesus; the expectation on the part of some that the world would soon come to an end did not give them any reason to preserve the story for future generations; and, compared with today, books were much more difficult and expensive to produce. A generation or more passed, therefore, before the books of the New Testament began to be written. Thus, in order to understand the New Testament in its original setting, we must trace, however briefly and inadequately, the origins and history of the Christian Church.

A central affirmation of Christianity has always been that while Jesus was put to death at the hands of sinful people, God raised him from the dead. Without belief in the Resurrection, the origin of the Christian Church is simply incomprehensible.

As Paul reminded the Corinthians, "If Christ has not been raised, then our preaching is in vain and your faith is in vain" (I Cor 15:14). The New Testament proclaims the Risen Christ on almost every page, but the main testimonies to the Resurrection are in I Cor 15:3-7 (where Paul passes on a very early tradition which he himself had received, presumably when he became a Christian) and in the closing sections of each of the four Gospels (Matt 28; Mark 16; Luke 24; John 20, 21). While there are differences of detail, all these accounts agree on the basic assertion: for Jesus, death was not the end. God raised him from the dead and he appeared to many of his followers, convincing them that he was gloriously alive. God had vindicated Jesus' claims and was now calling his followers to proclaim this good news to all who would listen.

Four Basic Convictions

For all their differences, the early Christians were firmly united in certain basic convictions which, of course, were meditated upon, expanded and elaborated in the course of time.

Firstly, they proclaimed the dawning of a *new age*. The God who had revealed himself in the Old Testament as Creator, Ruler, Judge and Saviour had now acted finally and decisively for our salvation. Again and again Christians searched the Old Testament and then showed how the prophecies had been fulfilled. Satan and the powers of evil had been struck a devastating blow. A major sign of the new age was the giving of the Holy Spirit in which all believers now shared. Of course, the old age still lingered on; the final judgment of evil and triumph of God's Kingdom still lay in the future. Nonetheless, the emphasis was primarily on the present: now was the day of salvation (II Cor 6:2), now was the climax and turning point of history, for the new age had already been inaugurated.

Secondly, Christians declared that this decisive act had happened in and through a *new servant* of God — in the birth, life, ministry, death and resurrection of Jesus. As it is often put, Jesus preached the Kingdom of God, but the Church preached Jesus; "the proclaimer became the proclaimed." Jesus may have been reticent about claiming the title Messiah, fearing that it would be taken in a political sense, but after his death and resurrection all possibility of misunderstanding was removed and Christians freely proclaimed that Jesus was indeed the Messiah, though not the kind of Messiah many people had been expecting. The Church strained to find terms adequate to express her understanding of who Jesus is: he is the Son of David and the true King; he is a prophet; he is a second Moses; he is the true High Priest; above all, he is the Servant of the Lord, prepared to suffer and give himself in the service of others. Titles like "Messiah" and "Son of man" which derived from the Old Testament and from Jewish tradition tended to fade into the background as Christianity spread outwards from Palestine into the wider Roman world. In their place other titles such as "Son of God" and "Lord," being more widely and readily understood, came to predominate. Special meaning was attached to Jesus' death as a sacrifice for the sins of the world and it was expected that, at the end, Jesus would come again in power and glory.

Thirdly, Christians believed in a *new community* which God had brought into existence. To the historian Christianity appears as an apocalyptic sect within Judaism. Christians themselves remembered that while Israel had been bound to God by the covenant at Mount Sinai, Jeremiah had seen the need for a "new covenant" (Jeremiah 31:31-34). Recalling how Jesus had referred to this passage as he took the bread and wine, symbols of his body and blood at his last supper with his disciples (I Cor 11:25), Christians saw Jesus' death as inaugurating the promised new covenant. The Church was in continuity with the old Israel, but it was also a new community. The mission to the Samaritans (Acts 8) accomplished at least symbolically the reunion of North and South foretold in the Old Testament (see Ezekiel 37:15-22), while the Gentile mission brought about the ingathering of the Gentiles, also foretold by the prophets (see Isaiah 45:22, 23). Christians shared a strong sense of community, and met regularly for worship. Entrance into the community was by baptism, and its life was nourished by the regular celebration of the Lord's Supper. Leadership was provided by the apostles and by prophets and others who were given gifts by the Holy Spirit.

Fourthly, the Church offered people a *new life*. Despite the deep sinfulness of human beings, a way of salvation was now offered through Christ. Through repentance and faith, believers could receive forgiveness and begin a new life in which they would be enabled to develop towards Christian maturity. Christians rejected legalism, preferring to stress the role of the Holy Spirit whose greatest gift is love. At the same time they found it necessary to produce guidelines to remind believers of the way of life they must follow. Christians rejected withdrawal from the world; they were to live in the world and to put their faith into practice in their daily lives and work, however difficult and demanding that might be. One of the strongest Christian beliefs was in the future resurrection of believers, yet here, too, the stress was on the present. Eternal life, the life of the new age, was not only a future hope; it could be experienced here and now.

In tracing the actual historical development of the early Church we have to work under some serious limitations. The Book of Acts is our major source and, while it does draw on earlier sources, its account is extremely sketchy and many parts of the Church's story are not dealt with at all. The letters of Paul shed light now and again on developments within the early Church, especially on certain events in which Paul himself was involved. The Gospels may tell us indirectly something about the communities in which and for which they and their sources were produced. We simply have to do the best we can with the limited source material at our disposal.

The Message Spreads

Acts focuses attention on Jerusalem where the giving of the Holy Spirit on the day of Pentecost fifty days after Jesus' crucifixion is what launches the Christian movement (Acts 2). Mark, Matthew and John know of resurrection appearances in Galilee, but the origin and development of the Church there is a mystery. The apostle Peter is portrayed as the initial leader of the Jerusalem community but, before long, we hear of a division between two groups, the "Hebrews" and the "Hellenists" (Acts 6). "Hebrews" refers to Jews who were Aramaic-speaking and this group is clearly the more conservative one, continuing to obey the Jewish Law and to worship in the Temple. The "Hellenists," on the other hand, were Greek-speaking Jews, some of whom may have returned after living abroad. The account of their leader Stephen, the first Christian martyr, suggests that they were the more radical group who saw no value in the Temple and who did not feel bound by all the provisions of the Law.

On Stephen's death the Hellenists fled Jerusalem, thus leaving the Hebrews to constitute the "mother church" of Christianity. After some time James, the brother of Jesus, apparently replaced Peter as the leader of the community. The fact that James, killed by Jewish authorities in the early 60s A.D., was replaced by Simeon, a cousin of Jesus, indicates that his family tie to Jesus was a primary factor in securing his acceptance as leader. The type of Christianity characteristic of the Jerusalem Church under James may be reflected in Matthew's Gospel and in the Letter of James, though most scholars today believe that both these works come from locations beyond Palestine.

Peter apparently became a roving missionary to Jewish communities in Palestine, perhaps in Asia Minor and in Corinth, and eventually in Rome where, according to tradition, he was martyred around A.D. 64. Peter's thought is reflected in I Peter. His later followers were probably responsible for Jude and II Peter.

The Hellenists, forced to leave Jerusalem, became active missionaries. Naturally, they spread the faith to other Greek-speaking Jews (Acts 11:19), but we find them breaking new ground with a mission to the Samaritans (Acts 8) and then making the big break-through with a mission to Gentiles (Acts 11:20). Thanks to them, Christianity ceased to be merely a sect of Judaism and began to develop as a universal faith accepting all those who responded to its message. The Hellenist Gentile mission established an important centre at Antioch in Syria. Many important developments occurred within Christianity as it spread to the great cosmopolitan cities of the Graeco-Roman world. The Letter to the Hebrews probably comes from a later stage of the Hellenist Jewish mission, and the Gospel and Letters of John may come from a group of Christian communities which can be traced back to the Hellenists.

In connection with the death of Stephen, Saul, later Paul, first appears on the scene. A Jew with a strict upbringing as a Pharisee, Paul also had a knowledge of Greek language and culture and, moreover, was a Roman citizen. It was on the road to Damascus, intent on hounding out the Christians there, that the zealous persecutor of the Church was transformed into a servant and apostle of Christ "in order that I might preach him among the Gentiles" (Gal 1:16). Paul is reticent in writing about his own religious experience, but Acts tells the story no fewer than three times (Acts 9:1-19; 22:3-16, 26:9-18). There are large gaps in our knowledge of Paul's early career; we can only guess what he did in his three year sojourn in Arabia (Gal 1:17) and in the period of perhaps ten years which he spent in Syria and Cilicia (Gal 1:21). The darkness starts to lift when we find the team of Barnabas and Paul working together at Antioch (Acts 11:25, 26).

At this point Acts narrates what are usually referred to as Paul's first, second and third missionary journeys (Acts 13, 14; 15:36-18:22; 18:23-21:16). These labels, however, are misleading in that Paul had travelled extensively before his "first" journey and also must have undertaken other travels not narrated in Acts. (For a reference to events, many of which are not recorded in Acts, see II Cor 11:23-27).

Paul became the great champion of the Gentile mission, but this development was not looked on with favour by all sections of the Church. More conservative Jewish-Christians wanted Gentiles to become proselytes or converts to Judaism first, to be circumcised and to accept the whole of the Law before they could become Christians. A major controversy developed, but on a visit to Jerusalem to confer with the leaders of the Church there, Paul and Barnabas won the support of both Peter and James for the view that Gentiles could be admitted without first becoming Jews (Gal 2:1-10). Another account of this "Council of Jerusalem" is found in Acts 15. Paul took this decision as the green light to embark on extensive missionary work in various parts of the Eastern Mediterranean area, although the controversy by no means ended overnight as Paul's Letter to the Galatians demonstrates. Paul's arrest in Jerusalem and his appeal to Ceasar, which resulted in his being sent to Rome for trial (Acts 21-28), brought his active missionary travels to a close. Paul's letters to the Thessalonians, the Corinthians, the Galatians and the Romans were written during his various travels, whereas his letters to the Philippians, the Colossians, Philemon, and the Ephesians were written while he was in prison.

We must never forget that Peter and Paul were not the only missionaries who spread the Christian message. When Paul reached Ephesus and, later on, Rome, he found in both cases a Church there ahead of him. We can only assume that many believers, whose names are completely unknown to us, helped to spread Christianity from city to city and from province to province.

Problems and Pressures — Without and Within

The middle and late 60s marked an important turning point in the history of the Church. From the Roman historian Tacitus we learn of the first persecution of Christians by the Roman state.[4] In A.D. 64 a great fire swept the city of Rome, and the Emperor Nero was suspected of having ordered it so that he could rebuild the city in grandiose fashion. Looking around for a convenient scapegoat, he fastened on the little-known group of Christians and had many of them cruelly tortured and put to death. Peter and Paul both probably perished in this outbreak of violence. Two years later nationalistic feeling in Palestine, which had been mounting for years, resulted in the outbreak of the great revolt of the Jews against the Romans. The fighting went on until the capture of Jerusalem and the destruction of the Temple in A.D. 70 (though a group of Zealots held out at the fortress of Masada until A.D. 73). Mark's Gospel was almost certainly written in Rome during these tumultuous years.

Inevitably, Christianity took some new directions after A.D. 70. For one thing, in this period Christianity became recognized as a religion clearly distinct from Judaism. So long as the Jerusalem Church led by the conservative James was in existence, strong links with Judaism were maintained. With the outbreak of the Jewish revolt the Jerusalem Christians fled to Pella in Transjordan. Thereafter, Jewish Christianity declined in numbers and influence. Gentile Christianity, on the other hand, flourished and became dominant. Some Christians viewed the capture of Jerusalem and the destruction of the Temple as a divine punishment on the Jewish people, thus inaugurating the long, unhappy history of unfriendly relations between Jews and Christians. Matthew's Gospel, Luke's Gospel and the Book of Acts, all written in this period, present the Christian Church as the true people of God.

This period also saw the beginning of sporadic persecution of the Church by the state. Judaism was a recognized religion with certain special privileges and, in the early decades of the Church, Christians were able to find shelter under the umbrella of Judaism. But, as soon as Christianity was seen as a separate religion, Christians became liable to suspicion and attack. We have noted the first such attack under Nero in A.D. 64. A further persecution probably took place under Domitian around A.D. 95; this is almost certainly the background of the Book of Revelation. A third outbreak occurred in Asia Minor in the reign of Trajan around A.D. 112.[5]

There were those in the early Church who expected the end of history and the return of Jesus to happen soon. The climactic events of the 60s, especially the destruction of the Jerusalem Temple, must have heightened expectations that the end was near. Yet, in the years after A.D. 70, life went on as usual. In this period we see a tendency to downplay belief in the end and to postpone the time of the end in Luke's Gospel and the Book of Acts. Nearer the end of the century the Gospel and letters of John re-interpret the earlier expectation and shift the emphasis from the future to the present. In times of opposition and persecution, however, hopes of an imminent end tended to resurface, and we find II Peter (probably the latest book of the New Testament) strongly reaffirming belief in the coming end.

The post-A.D. 70 period also saw false teaching becoming an increasing problem for the Church. Christians could easily recognize and brace themselves against opposition and attack from without but, sometimes, the more subtle threat of heresy within the Church proved to be even more dangerous. In the second century the movement known as "Gnosticism" posed a major threat to the Church. In the New Testament itself there are indications of tendencies which later manifested themselves in the full-blown Gnostic movement. This movement has been illuminated for us in recent years by the discovery of the Nag Hammadi codices in Egypt, many of which are Gnostic writings. The term "Gnosticism" comes from the Greek word *gnōsis* meaning "knowledge." Gnostics claimed to possess a special knowledge or revelation of secret doctrines known only to them. Typically, the Gnostics thought of themselves as a spiritual elite, superior to ordinary Christians. One of their basic beliefs was that matter and the human body are essentially evil; they found it difficult, therefore, to accept God as Creator of this world and also to believe that Jesus had truly become a human being. Their ethical views allowed them to go in one or other of two opposite directions: either a strict asceticism by which they sought to discipline themselves and bring the body into submission, or a licentiousness which claimed that the laws of morality did not apply to them. Paul encountered similar tendencies which the later books of the New Testament, such as I John, Jude and II Peter, strongly opposed.

Finally the 60s saw the death of Peter and Paul. While we know little or nothing about the fate of the other apostles, the original leaders of the Church were obviously removed one by one. Faced with increasing pressures and problems from without and within, the Church was forced to organize itself and to become much more of an institution than it had been in its earlier years. In I and II Timothy and Titus, in particular, we see the emergence of an ordered clergy with bishops, presbyters and deacons.

The history of the early Church is an exciting one. Placing the books of the New Testament in the setting of these movements and developments sheds much light on their making and meaning.

4.
The Formation of the New Testament

When we realize that the New Testament did not drop from heaven ready-made but consists of twenty-seven separate books written by various authors over a period of years, the question arises: How did these twenty-seven books come to be gathered together to form the "New Testament" which was added to the "Old Testament" to form the Christian Bible? Why these particular twenty-seven? Many other books circulated in the early Church. Why were they excluded? On what basis was the selection made?

This is what is known as the question of the *canon* of the New Testament. "Canon" comes from a Greek word which means a "reed" or "rod" or "stick." It can refer to what we call a rule or ruler, a piece of wood bearing a regular series of marks. From this comes the idea of a table or list. It can also be a tool used by builders or carpenters to check whether their work is straight or level. Applied to the Bible it has a double meaning: it signifies the *list* of books accepted by the Church as constituting sacred scripture, and it also means that these books are the *rule* or *standard* or *norm* by which the beliefs and practices of the Church are to be established and tested. Books which are on the list and which are regarded as authoritative are said to be "canonical"; all others are "non-canonical."

An approach developed by some scholars in recent years is known as "canonical criticism." It focuses on the process by which various books were gathered together to form the canon, and it stresses that what is important is the New Testament as it has been accepted by the Church over the years and as it is still used by the believing community in worship and as the rule of faith and life today.

A Gradual Process

Many people are surprised to discover that the formation of the canon of the New Testament was a long and gradual process. We have to remember that, for the early Christians, "Scripture" meant only the Old Testament which most of them would read in the Greek translation (generally known as the Septuagint). The books of the New Testament, of course, were not written until the second half of the first century A.D. and the earlier part of the second century. It took time for copies to be made, circulate and gradually become known to the growing Christian Church. Scholars have studied the writings of Christian authors of the second and third centuries in order to spot the earliest date at which each book of the New Testament is quoted; this indicates when they came to be in general circulation. After that, however, we have to try to determine when the books came to be regarded as authoritative and belonging to sacred Scripture. Lastly, we must establish when the list or canon was finally closed so that more books could be neither added nor taken away.

Two important Christian writers to note are the famous biblical scholar Origen (c. 185-254), and the great Church historian Eusebius (c. 260-340). Both of them indicated the books which were accepted in their day, others which were definitely not accepted, and a third category of "disputed" books on which opinions still differed. It is clear that by the early fourth century the question of the canon of the New Testament had still not been finally settled.

It is not too difficult to understand why, as time went on, some kind of canon became necessary. One factor may well have been the example of Marcion, a wealthy ship-owner from Asia Minor, who caused quite a commotion in the church at Rome around A.D. 140. Among other things he rejected the Old Testament and claimed that the God of the Old Testament was not the God revealed by Jesus. He issued a list of books which he considered authoritative. It consisted of one Gospel, that of Luke (carefully edited to remove whatever did not fit in with his ideas), along with ten letters by Paul. The Church definitely rejected Marcion's views but we can imagine Christians asking, in effect, "If Marcion's list of books is not the right one, what is?" As the Church became involved in the struggle with Gnosticism and, later, in the various theological controversies of the fourth century, it became more and more necessary for the Church to have a clear standard by which to determine the true faith.

Many other books circulated in the early Church in addition to the ones which were eventually accepted into the canon. Some of these are as early as, or even earlier than, some books of the New Testament. Examples include: the *First Letter of Clement*, written around A.D. 95 by Clement, the bishop of Rome, to the church at Corinth, appealing to the Christians there to heal the divisions which were plaguing their church and to demonstrate a spirit of humility and love; and the seven *Letters of Ignatius*, written about A.D. 107 by Ignatius, the bishop of Antioch, to various Christian churches as he was being taken to Rome to face a martyr's death; the *Epistle of Barnabas*, written some time between A.D. 70 and 150, which gives a Christian re-interpretation of the Old Testament; and the *Shepherd of Hermas*, dating from the early second century, in which the author relates a series of visions and discusses questions of Christian ethics. These books belong to the group generally known as the "Apostolic Fathers."[6] Some of them almost got into the New Testament, and none of them should be regarded as un-Christian or heretical.

Somewhat different are the books which make up what is generally referred to as the "Apocryphal New Testament."[7] It contains Gospels, Acts, Letters and Revelations, usually and falsely ascribed to apostles.

Almost all these books are definitely later in date than the New Testament. Many are works of fiction pure and simple, though it is quite possible that, here and there, some of them do preserve genuine early traditions. Among the more popular works were "infancy gospels" which sought to fill in the period of Jesus' childhood. The stories they contain are often quite ludicrous, like the account of how the young Jesus modelled some sparrows out of clay. Upon clapping his hands they turned into real sparrows and flew away! Some of these apocryphal books are quite harmless; others were clearly written to promote a point of view which the Church came to recognize as false and heretical.

Our knowledge of such works has been greatly expanded by the recent publication of a collection of books discovered near Nag Hammadi in Egypt.[8] These include such works as the *Gospel of Thomas*, the *Gospel of Philip*, and the *Gospel of Truth*. Most of these were associated with Gnosticism.

Their presence in Egypt, in the fourth century, in an area which was apparently a centre of Christian monasticism, suggests that clear-cut distinctions had not yet been made at that period.

Coming Together in Three Stages

It seems certain that the canon of the New Testament came into being in three stages. First of all, the letters of Paul were collected. In Col 4:16, Paul instructs the Christians at Colossae to exchange letters with another congregation. We can easily imagine how churches which had received letters from Paul would hear that he had also written to Rome and to Corinth, and so on, and would trade copies of their own letters for other ones. Many scholars believe that, in this way, a collection of the main letters of Paul existed by the year A.D. 90. However, the letters to Timothy and Titus do not appear in the earliest collections of Paul's letters, and the Letter to the Hebrews was certainly a problem: its authorship was obviously in doubt in the early centuries, and it was only with considerable misgivings that it was eventually tacked on to the collection of the letters of Paul.

The second part of the canon to come into being was the four Gospels. Originally, churches were probably content with one Gospel; Mark would be the Gospel of the church at Rome, for example, and Matthew that of the church at Antioch in Syria. Evidence suggests that by the middle of the second century the four had been collected together as a group. There do not seem to have been any serious problems with Matthew, Mark and Luke, but doubts about John's Gospel persisted until around A.D. 200. By the third century, however, the "fourfold Gospel" had become firmly established.

The third and last part of the New Testament to fall into place was the other letters and Revelation. Here, however, there was much more uncertainty. I Peter and I John were generally accepted from an early date, but various degrees of doubt attached to all the others — James, II Peter, II John, III John and Jude. Revelation caused special problems and was the last book accepted into the New Testament by Christians in the East.

The first list of the twenty-seven books which eventually became canonical is found in the Easter Letter of the Egyptian church leader, Athanasius, issued in 367. Before the end of that century, North African councils at Hippo (393) and Carthage (397) authorized lists of the twenty-seven books. However, the fact of the matter is that *no* council representing the whole Church *ever* ruled on the question. Instead, a consensus developed. It just became accepted that these were the twenty-seven books making up the New Testament. The Council of Trent in 1546 did list the books which constitute Scripture, but its rulings were binding on the Roman Catholic church only. On the Protestant side, Martin Luther did not regard all books of the New Testament as being of equal value. At one end of the scale he found the heart of the Christian message in John's Gospel, Paul's letters (especially Romans) and I Peter; at the other end, he questioned the value of Hebrews, James, Jude and Revelation, noting ancient doubts regarding their canonicity. In his translation of the New Testament into German, Luther did not put these works in their traditional place but relegated them to the very end of the New Testament. His doubts were soon forgotten, however, as the Protestant churches consolidated their position and, to this day. All Christians — Protestant, Roman Catholic and Orthodox alike — agree on which books make up the New Testament.

Closing the Canon

On what basis did this consensus develop? It is frequently said that the criterion for admission to the New Testament was authorship by one of the apostles but this is not really the case. For one thing, two of the four Gospels (Mark, Luke) were ascribed to writers who were definitely *not* apostles. For another thing, many of the apocryphal books claimed to be written by apostles but never did become part of the canon. In other words, a book was never accepted simply because it bore the name of an apostle; rather, a judgment had to be made on the basis of the book's contents.

It would be more accurate to say that a book was accepted if it contained "apostolic teaching," that is, teaching in accordance with the Gospel as preached by the apostles and their associates in the earliest days of the Church.

It is sometimes said that the books accepted were in general use in the Church's worship services Sunday by Sunday. There is truth in this but it is really just another way of saying that the canon was formed by a kind of general vote of the whole Church, spread over many years.

Of course, the Church did not see itself as conferring authority on the twenty-seven books but, rather, as recognizing the authority of God's word which was already inherent in them. Although the process was long and gradual, it is remarkable that the Church did reach complete unanimity on the canon of the New Testament. When the apocryphal books are examined, most people agree that the Church made a very wise choice in accepting the twenty-seven books which it did and in leaving the others out.

However, an often-asked question remains: Why should the canon of Scripture be closed at all? Why not add to the New Testament some of the classics of theology and devotion produced in later centuries? The answer lies in the central Christian conviction that the Christ event — the birth, life, death and resurrection of Jesus — constitutes God's final and decisive self-revelation, and the final and decisive action for our salvation.

The New Testament contains the primary witness to this unique event. Christian faith can and must be applied over and over again in new situations, and it can and must be translated into new languages and thought forms. However, the revelation given in Christ cannot itself be superceded or added to, for then it would no longer be a unique and final revelation. It is precisely here that the Christian Church has to part company with later sects and new religions which do accept the Bible but which *add* to it further writings of their own. If further revelation is necessary, then Christ is no longer the full and final revelation of God. For the Christian, therefore, the New Testament is the supreme authority for all matters of belief and conduct.

Having a canon does not mean, of course, that only these twenty-seven books are to be read! Christians can read with much profit the writings of the Apostolic Fathers, just as they may read Augustine's *Confessions* or Bunyan's *Pilgrim's Progress* or Barth's *Commentary on Romans* or Thomas Merton's *The Seven Storey Mountain.* But, for the Christian, neither these nor any other later books are ultimately authoritative. Everything Christians read is to be judged and evaluated in the light of God's supreme self-revelation in Jesus Christ. And for a knowledge of that revelation, Christians will always turn to the twenty-seven books which have for so long been recognized as constituting the canon of the New Testament.

5.
The Transmission of the New Testament

How can we be sure that the New Testament we read today accurately represents what was written by the original authors? How faithfully has the Greek text been preserved? For those who cannot read Greek, how accurate are the translations on which most modern readers must depend?

These are crucial considerations concerning the text because not one of the original copies of any of the books of the New Testament has survived and, although about five thousand manuscripts of the Greek New Testament are known to exist, most of these are copies of copies of copies of the original.

The books of the New Testament were written on papyrus, a material manufactured from the pith of the papyrus plant, a large reed which grows in water. For the first three centuries or so all copies of the books were also on papyrus. By about the early fourth century, papyrus began to be replaced as the main writing material by parchment or vellum which was prepared from animal skins by drying, stretching and smoothing them. Parchment folds more easily than papyrus and so was found to be particularly suitable for large books, especially when the desire arose to have the whole Bible in one volume. The scribes who copied the papyrus and then the parchment manuscripts of the New Testament used a form of capital letters known as "uncials." About the ninth century, perhaps because of the ever-growing demand for Bibles, scribes switched to a smaller, flowing style known as "minuscule" or "cursive" writing. This form prevailed until the introduction of printed New Testament texts in the sixteenth century. Thus manuscripts can be roughly dated by observing the material used and the style of handwriting.

Dealing with Copy Errors

Until the sixteenth century all manuscripts of the New Testament were copied by hand. Mistakes could easily creep in during the process of copying. No copy can ever be better than the original, but it can be very definitely inferior! When one scribe makes a series of mistakes in copying out a manuscript which is later copied by someone else, the second scribe will tend to copy the first scribe's mistakes and almost certainly add some more of his own. Mistakes thus tend to be cumulative.

Many of the errors made in copying the New Testament were quite unintentional. It was easy to confuse certain letters of the Greek alphabet which were quite similar in appearance and, of course, we must remember that in ancient manuscripts there was no space between words nor any punctuation. Sometimes a scribe skipped a whole line of the manuscript from which he was copying; this was easy to do, especially where two consecutive lines ended with the same word or phrase. Earnest students would write comments or notes in the margins of their New Testament and, when that manuscript was later copied, scribes would sometimes copy in the marginal notes thinking that they were part of the original text. In other cases, changes were made intentionally. Scribes corrected what they took to be errors in the spelling and grammar of earlier manuscripts. Sometimes they even omitted phrases or sentences which they found difficult to understand or with which they did not agree!

Whenever one manuscript differs from any other this is known as a "variant reading" or "variant." Such variants run into the tens of thousands. This is not as alarming as it sounds because the majority of these are fairly obvious mistakes which can be easily corrected. However, it is true that the first printed editions of the Greek New Testament in the sixteenth century were based on only a few manuscripts which were relatively late and obviously contained a very inferior form of text. These were the basis of what came to be called in the early 1600s the "Received Text" of the New Testament, a text which some people almost came to regard as itself divinely inspired! The situation changed with time, however, and in the nineteenth and twentieth centuries especially, the study of the text has been revolutionized by the discovery of much older and more reliable manuscripts.

Not until the last century, for example, did the two most valuable fourth century parchment uncial manuscripts became available to scholars: photographic facsimiles were published of the Codex Vaticanus, housed in the Vatican Library in Rome; and the Codex Sinaiticus was discovered in the Monastery of St. Catherine at the foot of Mount Sinai.

Until a century or so ago it was assumed that all of the papyrus manuscripts of the New Testament had been lost; however, a series of discoveries, mostly in the sands of Egypt, have made available about ninety papyrus manuscripts, although many of these are only fragmentary. Papyrus 52, published in 1935, is a fragment of a page of John's Gospel with John 18:31-33 on one side and John 18:37, 38 on the other; it was copied in the second century, perhaps about A.D. 125, and is the earliest surviving fragment of the New Testament. It is early enough to disprove completely the wild theories held by some radical nineteenth century scholars that John's Gospel was written as late as A.D. 150 or 160! In the 1930s, also, the Chester Beatty papyri were acquired, all of them dating from the third century and extremely valuable. These include Papyrus 45 with the Gospels and Acts, Papyrus 46 with part of Paul's letters, and Papyrus 47 with a section of Revelation. In the 1950s and early 1960s the Bodmer Papyri were published, including Papyrus 66 with parts of an early third century copy of John's Gospel and Papyrus 75, containing Luke and John, which was copied somewhere between A.D. 175 and 225.

Scholars can also make use of early translations of the New Testament into other languages to work out the Greek text from which these translations were made. The earliest ones are the versions in Latin and Syriac. A study of quotations of the New Testament in early Christian writings is also helpful since the place and approximate date of their composition can often be determined.

Altogether there is a mass of material with which to work. New discoveries are constantly being made and newly found manuscripts being added to the list. It should be noted that both the quantity and the quality of the manuscript evidence for the Greek New Testament are far superior than for any other book which has come down to us from the ancient world: the surviving manuscripts of a number of the Greek and Roman literary classics can be counted on the fingers of one hand.

The textual scholar aims to reconstruct as accurately as possible the original text of each book of the New Testament. This is an enormous task to which many scholars have devoted the work of a lifetime. For any given book it is necessary to compare as many manuscripts as possible and, where there are variant readings, to decide which reading is most likely to be the original one. This cannot be determined simply by counting the manuscripts and following the reading favoured by the majority, since the bulk of the surviving manuscripts are relatively late and contain many errors and revisions. A seemingly obvious approach would be to choose the reading found in the earliest surviving manuscript. This is certainly an important general principle, but the matter is not as simple as that! Some of the papyri came from a very early period when the text was evidently still copied with a degree of freedom, whereas a mediaeval manuscript might have been copied, let us say, from a fourth century parchment uncial manuscript which preserved a very accurate type of text.

Although there are no fool-proof rules, scholars have developed some guidelines to follow. One is to "prefer the shorter reading," since later copyists tended to add to and expand the text. Another is to "prefer the more difficult reading," since scribes usually tried to smooth out difficulties and eliminate problems. It has been discovered that similar sets of readings are found in whole groups of manuscripts, and this has led to the identification of certain "families." From these a kind of "family" tree can be constructed in which some branches are obviously later, whereas others are nearer the original "trunk" of the tree.

What difference does it all make? Let us take an example. In Rev 1:5, in the second part of the verse, the writer ascribes glory and dominion to the risen Christ, referring to "him that loved us, and washed us from our sins in his own blood..." That, at least, is what we read in the *King James Version.* The Greek word for "washed" is *lousanti,* a participle from the verb *louō* which means to "wash," but this reading is found only in later manuscripts. We now know that three parchment manuscripts of the fourth and fifth centuries as well as Papyrus 18 of the third or fourth century read *lusanti.* This is only one letter different, but *lusanti* comes from another verb, *luō,* which means to "loose" or "untie" or "set free." The evidence strongly favours this reading which is followed by most modern translations such as the *Revised Standard Version.* It reads, "To him who loves us and *has freed us* from our sins by his blood..." Rev 7:14 does refer to the saints in heaven as having "washed their *robes* and made them white in the blood of the Lamb," but Revelation does not refer to Christians themselves as having been "washed in the blood." What is said is that through the blood or death of Jesus, Christians have been *set free* from sin.

One of the most famous examples of a variant reading is found in I John 5:7, 8 where the *King James Version* refers not only to the threefold witness of Spirit, water and blood (referring to Jesus' baptism and crucifixion, or perhaps to Christian baptism and the Lord's Supper) but also states: "There are three that bear record in heaven, the Father, the Word, and the Holy Ghost: and these three are one." This sounds like a clear reference to the doctrine of the Trinity, to God as Father, Son (or Word) and Holy Spirit, one God in three persons. But these words are not found in any Greek manuscript earlier than the sixteenth century! They were added as a marginal note or comment in an early Latin copy of the New Testament. Sometime about the fifth century they began to be copied into Latin manuscripts and eventually found their way into copies of the Latin Vulgate translation from about the ninth century onwards. These words came to be accepted as authentic and appeared in the "Received Text" and so in the *King James Version.* Today, virtually all scholars recognize that they are not part of the original text, and any reputable modern translation omits them. Needless to say, Christian belief in the Trinity in no way stands or falls on the basis of this text; there are numerous other New

Testament references to God as Father, as Son, and as Holy Spirit.

These cases are interesting examples of variant readings, but they can be misleading if they give the impression that there are many variant readings in the manuscripts of the New Testament which could have a bearing on basic Christian beliefs. The great majority of variants concern only minor questions of grammar or spelling and, even when they relate to more important matters, we can today, in the greater number of cases, be reasonably certain what the original text read.

Recent years have seen increasing participation by Roman Catholic scholars in work on the text, and full co-operation between Protestants and Roman Catholics now exists. Modern tools, such as the computer, are increasingly used to handle the vast amount of data. The leading editions of the Greek New Testament are the popular "Nestle-Aland" version, edited by outstanding German scholars, and the United Bible Societies' text, edited by an international committee of leading experts. There has been growing co-operation on the part of the scholars involved and the 26th edition of Nestle-Aland, published in 1979, adopted exactly the same Greek text as the third edition of the United Bible Societies (1975). Thanks to the labours of these and many earlier scholars, we have today a text of the Greek New Testament which does not differ greatly — and certainly not on any essential points — from the originals written so many centuries ago.

Modern Translations Are Preferable

The demand for translations of the New Testament is not only a modern one. Although Greek was widely spoken in the Eastern Mediterranean area at the time of the birth of Christianity, the need for a Latin version was felt by the second century. This "Old Latin" translation, as it is called, was revised in the late fourth century by the famous biblical scholar Jerome, and combined with his version of the Old Testament to constitute the Latin *Vulgate* or "common" version which was the Bible of Western Christendom for over a thousand years. Almost as old as the earliest Latin translation was a version in Syriac. As Christianity grew and spread, other translations were called for in such languages as Egyptian Sahidic and Bohairic, Gothic, Armenian, Georgian, Slavonic and so on.

There were some attempts to translate the New Testament into early forms of the English language. The Venerable Bede, who worked in the monastery at Jarrow in the north of England and who died in 735, is credited with a translation of John's Gospel. In mediaeval times the Church discouraged translations designed for general use, so the first complete translation of the Bible into English was the work of John Wycliffe (1330? - 1384), often known as "The Morning Star of the Reformation" because he anticipated a fundamental principle of the Protestant Reformation, namely, that the Bible should be made available in the language of the people. This aim inspired William Tyndale (1492? - 1536) whose translation, made from the original Greek, strongly influenced later versions. Tyndale paid with his life for making this translation; with his dying breath he prayed, "Lord, open the King of England's eyes." His prayer was answered when the king (Henry VIII) did change his mind and supported the publication of the *Coverdale Bible* in 1535 (the work of Miles Coverdale) and *Matthew's Bible* in 1537. These were followed by the *Great Bible* (1539), the very popular *Geneva Bible* (1560) and the *Bishop's Bible* (1568).

It was partly the multiplication of translations, partly the fact that each had notes with varying theological interpretations, that prompted James, who had just become king of England as well as Scotland, to summon a conference of scholars in 1604 and embark on a project to produce a new version which could be used throughout the land. Scholars were expected to consult the existing translations in the process but to produce a new one without any notes. The *King James Version,* named for its sponsor, appeared in 1611. It is also known as the *Authorized Version,* although no record has survived of how it was officially authorized. The original title page did bear the words, "Appointed to be Read in Churches." In opposition to the various Protestant translations, Roman Catholic scholars produced the *Douai-Rheims Version* of the New Testament in 1582 (with the Old Testament in 1610), though it was not intended for general use by the laity; it underwent a whole series of revisions.

In time the *King James Version* became the standard and, indeed, for Protestants, the only Bible in English; it was reprinted over and over again, although not without certain changes. Not until 1881 was it felt necessary to produce an official revision, the *Revised Version*. Even then, it was a very conservative and tame revision. Only slightly different was the *American Standard Version* of 1901.

It is really only in the twentieth century that the need has been felt for either a much more thorough revision or, increasingly, for completely new modern translations. Why not be content with the *King James Version*, the greatest piece of literature in the English language? Firstly, the *King James Version* was made from the "Received Text" of the Greek New Testament which, as we have seen, was based on a relatively few, mainly rather late, manuscripts. Modern translations can take advantage of the much earlier and better manuscripts discovered in the nineteenth and twentieth centuries and so are based on a Greek text which is much closer to the original.

Secondly, our knowledge of the Greek language has improved tremendously thanks to continuing study as well as to new discoveries. Numerous secular papyri written around New Testament times have come to light which show that the Greek of the New Testament was not the literary language used by writers and scholars but, for the most part, the common (or *Koinē*) Greek, the language of everyday life and of the marketplace. The ongoing study of language also continues to shed new light. For example, John 4:9 in the *King James Version* declares that "the Jews have no dealings with the Samaritans." The meaning of the verb used *(sunchraomai)* is uncertain but, in 1950, a scholarly article argued convincingly that what it means here is "to use together."[9] This makes sense of the passage; Jesus asks the Samaritan woman for a drink of water, and he could have got this only by using the woman's water jar which practicing Jews would certainly not do because they regarded Samaritans as ritually unclean. This argument has been accepted in a number of recent translations such as the *New English Bible* which translates, "Jews and Samaritans, it should be noted, do not use vessels in common."

A third reason for using a modern translation is that the English language itself has changed considerably since 1611;

many older words have become obsolete or else have changed their meaning. For example, in I Cor 7:32 Paul tells his readers that he would have them "without carefulness." Why so? Is it not a good thing to be careful? In 1611 "careful" meant "full of care" or anxiety, and the meaning is correctly conveyed by modern translations which read, "I want you to be free from anxieties" (*Revised Standard Version*), or "I would like you to be free from worry" (*Today's English Version*).

One of the most widely used modern versions is the *Revised Standard Version,* a far-reaching revision of the *American Standard Version* (hence a revision of a revision of the *King James Version)* based on the latest modern discoveries and scholarship. The New Testament was published in 1946 (and the Old Testament in 1952). With some very minor changes it has been accepted by the Roman Catholic and Orthodox churches in the form of the *Common Bible* or *Revised Standard Version: An Ecumenical Edition* (1973), and it has been widely used in recent years by conservative Protestants as well as liberals; hence, it is the one modern version accepted by almost all branches of the Christian Church. It is subject to continuing revision.

Completely new translations of the New Testament into modern English were pioneered by such persons as the Scottish scholar James Moffatt in 1913, and the American scholar Edgar J. Goodspeed in 1923. Since then there has been a flood of new translations. The *New English Bible* (New Testament, 1961) was commissioned by the major Protestant churches of Great Britain; as well as biblical scholars, literary experts were employed to advise on the most appropriate English style. There has been an increasing trend away from literal, word-for-word translations towards finding the "dynamic equivalent" of the original Greek in modern English. The best example of this approach is the New Testament in *Today's English Version* (also known as *Good News for Modern Man*) published in 1966; along with the Old Testament it was published as the *Good News Bible* in 1976 by the United Bible Societies. Over fifty million copies of the New Testament have been sold. The *New International Version* (1973), sponsored by conservative Protestants, is another completely new translation; it aims to be faithful to the original languages and to avoid paraphrasing. Many readers have appreciated the paraphrases of the New

Testament by J. B. Phillips, brought together as *The New Testament in Modern English* (1958); this approach can be helpful, provided it is realized that this is a paraphrase rather than an exact translation.

The twentieth century has seen a dramatic change in the attitude of the Roman Catholic church with new translations into English such as the *Westminster Version* (1913-1935) and that by Ronald A. Knox (1944). The encouragement of biblical studies by the papal encyclical *Divino Afflante Spiritu* in 1943 and the stress on making the Bible available in the language of the people at Vatican II helped to produce the *Jerusalem Bible* in 1966 (a revised edition, *The New Jerusalem Bible* was published 1985) and the *New American Bible* in 1970.

The *King James Version* will always have a unique place in the history of English language and literature and, no doubt, also in the hearts of many Christians. But those who wish a clear and accurate knowledge of what the original authors of the New Testament wrote should turn to a reliable modern translation.

PART II

THE BOOKS OF THE NEW TESTAMENT

6.
The Letters to the Thessalonians and the Philippians

The fact that the books of the New Testament are not listed in the order in which they were written can easily make us forget that the earliest part of the New Testament consists of the letters of Paul.

Missionary Travels and the Need for Follow-up

As we have already noted, our knowledge of Paul's early years as a Christian is sketchy. From chapter 13 onwards, however, the Book of Acts obviously has access to sources which provide a quite detailed account of some of Paul's missionary travels, starting with a journey to Cyprus and Asia Minor, followed some time later by a longer journey through Asia Minor, then crossing over into Europe and travelling south through Macedonia and Greece. At many locations Paul established Christian churches, then moved on. As we can well imagine, this created problems of "follow-up" in the newly established Christian congregations. Paul could not be everywhere at once. Though he was not always able to go back in person, he had two means of helping his churches. In the first place, he could use a younger assistant such as Timothy to visit congregations and to deal with crises which had arisen. Secondly, he could write letters to his churches — and Paul was one of the greatest letter writers of all time. His opponents at Corinth did not think much of him as a preacher but even they had to admit that "his letters are weighty and strong" (II Cor 10:10).

Most of Paul's letters follow a similar pattern based on the format which was standard at the time: an *opening* which identifies the sender and the recipients and sends greetings; a prayer of *thanksgiving;* the main *body* of the letter; words of *exhortation;* and a *closing* with personal greetings and final words of blessing. Paul's letters were intended to be read out to the assembled Christian congregation, as I Thess 5:27 shows. Although he wrote most of his letters to particular churches to deal with quite specific problems, Paul always dealt with each individual case in the light of his understanding of the Christian message as a whole. Indeed, it must have been apparent that the letters contained much that could be valuable to other Christians in different situations. This is undoubtedly why Paul's letters were preserved, collected and eventually embodied in the New Testament so that, through them, God's Word might speak to subsequent generations and indeed to Christians today.

According to Acts 16 and 17, when Paul crossed over into Europe he established congregations in three of the major cities of Macedonia — Philippi, Thessalonica and Beroea. The briefest account concerns the visit to Beroea and we know nothing further of the fortunes of the church there. But Paul later had occasion to write letters to the Christians in the other two cities, to those at *Philippi* (the Philippians) and to those at *Thessalonica* (the Thessalonians).

Paul's letters to the Thessalonians are probably the earliest writings in the New Testament. Acts 17:1-9 gives a short but vivid account of Paul's visit to Thessalonica, along with his associate Silas (or Silvanus) and his assistant Timothy. He began preaching in the local synagogue but had little success there. Evidently most of the Thessalonian converts were Gentiles. No sooner had the infant congregation been established than it faced severe opposition from the local Jewish population. Paul and his companions apparently went into hiding, but his host, Jason, was brought before the magistrates and had to give security for the good conduct of his guests. In the circumstances it was thought advisable for Paul and his friends to leave, so they slipped away by night to Beroea.

The Future Life and the End Time

I Thessalonians, apart from the brief opening greeting in 1:1 and the closing greeting in 5:23-28, falls clearly into two main parts. In the first, (1:2 — 3:13) Paul looks back at these events with a mixture of joy and sorrow — joy at the establishment of a loyal and faithful Christian congregation, but sorrow at the fact that he had to leave them in a time of crisis. Paul was worried sick at what was happening in Thessalonica. He dearly wanted to go back but this did not prove possible (I Thess 2:17, 18). From Beroea he had gone on to Athens. Once there, however, he could stand it no longer, so he sent Timothy back to Thessalonica (I Thess 3:1, 2). We can sense the anxiety and apprehension with which Paul awaited Timothy's return, and there is no mistaking the relief and rejoicing with which he greeted the news when it eventually did come. "Now that Timothy has come to us from you, and has brought us the good news of your faith and love... we have been comforted... for now we live, if you stand fast in the Lord" (I Thess 3:6-8). It is probable that by the time Timothy got back, Paul had moved on to Corinth (Acts 18:5), so I Thessalonians would be written from there.

Paul wrote to let the Thessalonians know how he felt and to encourage them in the face of continuing difficulties. In the second half of his letter (I Thess 4, 5) he takes the opportunity to give some advice and, in particular, to discuss a matter which had been bothering the Thessalonians (presumably Timothy had brought back word on this).

Paul's proclamation of the Christian message must certainly have included the hope and the assurance of a future life for believers. This was expressed in terms taken over from Judaism: history as we know it will come to an end, God will usher in a completely new order, the dead will be raised (the resurrection), and the faithful will enjoy the life of the new age. For Christians these events are associated with the "coming" (the Greek word is *parousia*) of the Lord, i.e. the return or Second Coming of Christ. Some in the early Church expected this to happen soon. Paul himself at this point apparently envisaged it as happening within his lifetime, as I Thess 4:15 shows ("we who are alive, we who are left until the coming of the Lord").

The Thessalonians had evidently misunderstood Paul and expected the end to come very soon indeed. But in the interval since Paul left them, one or two members of the congregation had died, and the Thessalonians were worried as to whether their departed loved ones would miss out on the future life since they would not be alive at Christ's return.

Paul writes a careful and sympathetic reply. First, he assures his readers that they have no need to worry: Christian hope applies to the dead just as much as to the living. He reminds them of the events expected to happen at the end, with the resurrection of the dead being an important part. Secondly, in line with the teaching of Jesus, he emphasizes that the Christian view is not that the end will come *soon,* but that it will come *suddenly* (see I Thess 5:1-11 and compare Matt 24:43, 44 and Luke 12:39, 40). The end will come "like a thief in the night." We have probably all encountered or at least heard of people who claim to be able to predict the time of the end of the world, basing their calculations on various passages in Daniel and Revelation. 1914 and 1984 were favourite dates with some groups, but when such prophecies are not fulfilled, they revise their calculations and come up with a new date, nothing daunted. How are we to cope with such people if they come knocking on our door? The best way by far is to point to the clear teaching of the New Testament itself. Jesus said that even he did not know the time of the end (Mark 13:32), and here Paul stresses that Christians are not to spend their time awaiting the end and still less calculating the time of the end; rather, they are to go about their daily tasks faithfully and lovingly, in a state of constant preparedness to give an account of themselves whenever they may be called upon to do so.

Finally, it is noteworthy that while Paul gives a brief outline of the end-events, he makes no effort to describe the future life. It is only natural that people would speculate about what lies beyond death. In some civilizations tools, weapons and even food were buried with the dead, suggesting that the future was seen more or less as a re-run of this life. The New Testament is characterized by two emphases: by the *certainty* of its belief in a future resurrection, and by a *reticence* to go into details. There is very little interest in "the furniture of heaven or the temperature of hell." Following the lead of Jesus himself (cf. Luke 23:43)

Paul is content with words which have brought comfort to countless believers: "... so we shall always be with the Lord" (I Thes 4:17). If Christians know that after death they shall be with Christ, they know all they need to know.

The Long-term Struggle between Good and Evil

II Thessalonians is quite similar in some ways to I Thessalonians and even echoes some of its wording, yet it seems less friendly in tone and contains teaching different from that found in the first letter. Some scholars have doubted whether Paul wrote II Thessalonians, but there is little to commend this theory. There are no serious problems in supposing that not long after he wrote I Thessalonians, Paul got word of further problems in the church at Thessalonica. Despite what Paul had written in his first letter, some of the Christians there were so excited by the expectation of the imminent end of the world that they had given up working. After all, if the end is to come any day what is the point of continuing to work? The situation seems to have been aggravated, perhaps, by someone who had misled the Thessalonians and certainly by what must have angered and frustrated Paul — a letter sent to Thessalonica by someone else, but purporting to have been written by Paul. (See II Thess 2:2, and note how careful Paul is to authenticate this letter with his own signature in II Thess 3:17).

It is not surprising, then, that Paul dashed off another letter, perhaps not too long after the first and probably while he was still in Corinth. While he encourages the readers to hold fast under continuing opposition and persecution, his main purpose is to dampen the over-excitement of those expecting an imminent Second Coming and to help the Thessalonians put the Christian hope for the future in a proper perspective.

On the practical level, Paul emphasizes again that Christians must serve God in their daily lives and in their daily work. "If any man will not work, let him not eat" (II Thess 3:10). For many people today, work is a necessary evil or even a curse. Paul's discussion assumes that people should work (and should have a job to work at) and that they should find satisfaction in their work. For Christians work is not a curse: it is the God-given means of providing for their own needs and for the needs of others.

On another level, Paul expands his teaching on the future, once again drawing on ideas taken over from Judaism (II Thess 2:1-12). The end cannot be imminent because certain events must *precede* the end, in particular, an intensification of the struggle between good and evil in the world. There will be a final rebellion against God led by the Anti-Christ, "the lawless one," although for the time being the forces of evil are being held in check by the restraining hand or "restrainer," by which Paul probably means the Roman Empire. Many people today still believe that the world can get better and better by human effort; the New Testament holds that things will get worse before they get better. Of course, Christians believe in the ultimate triumph of God, but so long as history lasts, the struggle between good and evil will continue and even intensify. There is profound truth here, for the twentieth century as well as for the first.

Christian Joy, Unity and Service

The other Macedonian church to which Paul wrote was *Philippi* where he first preached the Gospel on crossing over into Europe. Acts 16:12-40 tells in some detail of his visit there: of the conversion of the business woman Lydia, of his healing of an exploited slave girl, of the imprisonment and escape of Paul and Silas, and of the conversion of the jailor.

When and where Paul wrote this letter we cannot be sure. Certainly, at the time of writing, he was in prison (Phil 1:7, 13, 14, 17). Traditionally, this has been taken to refer to his final imprisonment at Rome (in the early 60s A.D.); however, Caesarea, where Paul spent two years in prison in the late 50s, and Ephesus, in the mid-50s, are other possibilities championed by some scholars. Fortunately these uncertainties in no way detract from the message of the letter.

Of all the churches founded by Paul, Philippi was the one with which he had the warmest relationship. The Philippians had voluntarily and gladly continued to share in Paul's work after he had left them by sending gifts to him in Thessalonica and then to other locations (Phil 4:15, 16). More recently, they had sent help again by Epaphroditus who, unfortunately, had become seriously ill while with Paul. He has now recovered and probably it is he who carries the letter back to Philippi. Paul commends him for his faithfulness and seems to want to make sure that he is well received on his return (Phil 2:25-30, 4:18).

The dominant note is one of joy. This is not the superficial, forced-smile, slap-on-the-back type of emotion we encounter in some so-called Christians or see on some TV shows. It is rather "joy in the Lord." It is the joy that lights up the face of Mother Theresa despite the lines inflicted by the world's suffering and need. It is the joy that arises from a common commitment to Jesus Christ and to the work of his Church and from a true Christian fellowship which has stood the test of time.

This mood is broken sharply at 3:2 which introduces a section in which Paul lashes out at opponents who were threatening to disrupt the Philippian church — "Look out for the dogs." So violent is the change that some scholars have suggested that chapter 3 was originally part of another letter by Paul. While this may be possible, it is not necessarily the case: in a personal letter changes of mood are not uncommon, and it is even possible that while he was writing, fresh news reached Paul of persons causing trouble at Philippi. These people evidently wanted Gentile Christians to observe all the details of the Jewish Law, but it is not clear whether they were Jews or Jewish-Christians of some description.

Paul also wrote to appeal for unity. Two women within the church had had a disagreement (Phil 4:2). What would Euodia and Syntyche have said if they had known that this is what their names would be remembered for? It is Paul's appeal for reconciliation and unity (Phil 1:27) which calls forth the greatest passage in the letter, the "Christ Hymn" of 2:6-11. Possibly Paul is quoting an early Christian hymn, for the passage is in the form of poetry and contains a number of words not found elsewhere in Paul. To a practical problem, people "not getting along" with each other within a congregation, Paul brings the profoundest theological statement. Christ had divine status but he was willing to "empty" himself by becoming a human being. Humbly he became the servant of others in complete obedience to God, even when that obedience led to the cross. Christ's exaltation as "Lord" came only through humble and self-sacrificing service. Christian congregations should be models of community, examples of unity despite diversity. Yet, how often do disagreements and resentments arise within congregations, often for the most trivial reasons — someone is accidentally left out of the vote of thanks, or someone else is not asked to pour tea. Neither individuals nor congregations will get very far in the Christian life until they learn to share this attitude which was in Christ Jesus. Only when they are willing to empty themselves in the service of others will they be able to share the fellowship and the joy that characterized Paul's relations with the Philippians.

7. The Letters to the Corinthians

It has become very fashionable to stress the differences between the world of the New Testament and the world we live in today, the implication usually being that there is little in the New Testament that is directly applicable to our day and age. While there is some truth in this view, it can be taken too far. Glance down a list of some of the topics Paul discusses in I Corinthians: divisions within the church; should Christians participate in lawsuits?; sex outside of marriage; sex within marriage; divorce; mixed marriages; do women have to wear hats in church?; the meaning of the Lord's Supper; what happens if some of your congregation join the charismatic movement?; are women preachers allowed?; is there life after death?; why is the church always asking for money? Many of these topics are still capable today of arousing lively interest if not controversy!

Even when Paul is discussing a subject which is completely foreign to us, such as whether or not it is right to eat meat which was originally part of a sacrifice to pagan gods, he bases his advice on principles which can be applied in quite different circumstances. When we add to this the fact to which II Corinthians bears ample testimony, namely, that many people in the Corinthian church spent a great deal of their time criticizing their minister, we may well ask whether the situation in first century Corinth was really so different from our situation today!

Corinth: A Source of Heartaches for Paul

After founding the churches at Philippi and Thessalonica, and after a visit to Athens, Paul went on to Corinth. Acts 18:1-18 gives only the sketchiest account, especially when we remember that Paul spent at least a year and a half there (Acts 18:11). Corinth was a large cosmopolitan city strategically located on the narrow isthmus which links northern and southern Greece. A centre of transportation and commerce, it had a distinctly unsavoury reputation. I Cor 6:9-11 gives a thumbnail sketch of the kind of background from which some of the Corinthian converts came: "Do not be deceived: neither the immoral, nor idolators, nor adulterers, nor homosexuals, nor thieves, nor the greedy, nor drunkards, nor revilers, nor robbers will inherit the kingdom of God. And such were some of you." I Cor 1:26 indicates that few Christians came from the upper or better educated classes.

It was in such a city that Paul proclaimed the Good News and established a congregation which flourished but would also cause him all kinds of headaches and heartaches. After leaving Corinth Paul kept in regular touch with the church there. Almost certainly the whole correspondence between Paul and Corinth has not survived, although many scholars believe that what we call "II Corinthians" contains parts of more than one letter: when copies were being made of Paul's letters it is quite easy to understand how several shorter ones might have been copied out together on the one scroll.

When he left Corinth Paul returned to Palestine and then went to Ephesus on the west coast of Asia Minor where he made his headquarters for the next few years. In I Cor 5:9 Paul says, *"I wrote to you in my letter* not to associate with immoral persons." Clearly this means that Paul had already written a letter to Corinth *before* he wrote I Corinthians. This earlier letter has not survived, although some scholars think that II Corinthians 6:14 — 7:1 might have been part of it. That section looks very like an insertion breaking the sense between 6:13 and 7:2, and the subject matter is precisely the need to separate from unbelievers. There are a number of parallels between this section and the Dead Sea Scrolls, and, possibly, Paul was quoting from an Essene source.

Following this earlier letter Paul received news of what was happening in Corinth from two sources: a report brought by "Chloe's people" (I Cor 1:11) and a letter from the Corinthians asking for guidance on a series of problems (I Cor 7:1). In answer to these Paul wrote I Corinthians. He probably had Timothy take the letter to Corinth (see I Cor 4:7, 16:10, 11).

At this point the situation apparently deteriorated, and we have to assume that Paul paid a flying visit to Corinth in an effort to put matters to rights. Although this visit is not mentioned in Acts, Paul himself, in II Corinthians, refers back to a "painful visit" (II Cor 2:1; 12:14, 13:1). This visit does not seem to have been successful, so when he got back to Ephesus, Paul decides to write again to Corinth in the most severe terms. "I wrote you out of much affliction and anguish of heart and with many tears... Even if I made you sorry with my letter, I do not now regret it..." (II Cor 2:4, 7:8). There is a great deal to be said for the view that our II Corinthians 10 to 13 formed part of that "severe letter." The tone of II Corinthians 1 to 9 is warm and friendly, but there is a complete change at the beginning of chapter 10. Chapters 10 to 13 consist of a fierce defence of Paul's apostleship along with an equally fierce attack on "false apostles" who had been causing havoc in the Corinthian church.

This severe letter was taken to Corinth by Titus and, typically, Paul was overcome with anxiety. He could not wait for Titus to get back but started out to meet him, going the length of Macedonia where he did meet Titus (II Cor 7:5-7; cf. Acts 20:1). The news was good, for the crisis was over and Paul's authority at Corinth re-established. In relief and joy over the reconciliation Paul wrote II Corinthians (or II Cor 1-9 if we believe that II Cor 10-13 is part of the earler severe letter). Not long after, Paul travelled south into Greece (Acts 20:2, 3) and paid his last visit to Corinth; hopefully, it was a happy one.

From this complicated timetable of events one thing at least will be obvious: the letters, which we call I and II Corinthians, are not carefully polished academic treatises on theology but, rather, were written in quite specific crisis situations, often in the heat of controversy and in agony of heart.

We can imagine Paul pacing up and down, dictating I Corinthians, dealing in chapters 1 to 6 with the problems reported by Chloe's people, then in chapters 7 to 15 answering the Corinthians' questions, ticking them off his list one by one — "Now concerning the matters about which you wrote..." (I Cor 7:1; cf. 7:25, 8:1, 12:1, 16:1).

The Nature and Image of the Church

It seems that there was a group of people within the Corinthian church who were arrogant and boastful: they claimed a superior "wisdom" and "knowledge"; they claimed to be specially endowed with the Spirit; with their slogan "All things are lawful" (I Cor 6:12) they claimed the right to behave as they pleased; they were the "spiritual ones," distinctly superior to ordinary Christians. They may have been the party who claimed, "I belong to Apollos" (I Cor 1:12). Others claimed the authority of Cephas (i.e. Peter), and still others of Paul himself. Patiently, Paul explains the very basis of the Church. Cleverness, social status, influence — none of these things can put one Christian on a higher level than another in a community which originated with a crucified Messiah. Wordly standards simply do not apply within the Church. Christian leaders are not to be seen as rivals but as fellow-workers under God. "I planted," says Paul, "Apollos watered, God gave the growth" (I Cor 3:6). Changing the illustration, the Church is like a structure which all believers have a hand in building; what counts is that they build on the one foundation, Jesus Christ (I Cor 3:11). What a rebuke these chapters are to the dissensions ranging from the personal to the denominational, which still rack the Church today. No wonder non-believers are so often turned off! What counts is not that "I am of Luther" or "I am of Calvin" or "I am of Wesley," not even "I am a Protestant," "I am a Catholic" or "I am Orthodox"; what counts is that first, last and all the time the Christian's loyalty should be to Christ himself.

In discussing a case of blatant immorality within the congregation which the Corinthians were complacently ignoring (I Cor 5:1-13, 6:9-20), and in appealing to Christians to settle disputes among themselves without going to (pagan) courts (I Cor 6:1-8), Paul has an important concern in mind: what kind of "image" does the Church project to outsiders? Even pagans did not allow the kind of immorality found within the Corinthian church. What will unbelievers think if Christians defraud and then sue one another? How often do we hear people today asking, "Why should I be a member of the Church? Professing Christians are no better than anyone else." People in our society often fail to see any difference between Christians and non-Christians. In an age when the Church often seems to fail to give a clear lead on moral questions, when "situation ethics" are apparently taken by some to mean that almost anything goes, can the Church claim to have a lifestyle that is truly distinctive? Today, governments, business and labour are greatly concerned about the "image" they project to the general public. The Church has to be concerned about its image, too, and that image depends largely on how individual Christians live their lives from day to day.

Laying Down Basic Principles

Paul's discussion in chapter 7 of relations between the sexes has caused problems for many people. It may help to realize that Paul is probably countering a group which held that Christians should abstain from sexual relationships altogether. If that is so, then the most important thing is Paul's reaffirmation of the God-given nature of marriage and of sexual relations within marriage. Some, like Paul himself, have been called by God to remain unmarried and, while Paul sees that such persons may have greater freedom to devote themselves to the Lord's work, there is *no* claim that the unmarried state is superior to the married.

In studying Paul's discussion on this and other controversial points, such as whether women should cover their heads during worship (I Cor 11:2-16) and whether women should be allowed to preach (I Cor 14:33-35), two points should be kept in mind.

The first is that where Paul can quote a saying of Jesus, as on the matter of divorce (I Cor 7:10, 11), that settles the question: the Christian ideal is the life-long union of husband and wife. He clearly separates from this his advice on other questions: "Now concerning the unmarried, I have no command of the Lord, but I give my opinion..." (I Cor 7:25; cf. 7:12). Of course, he does add that in these judgments, "I think that I have the Spirit of God" (I Cor 7:40).

The other point to note is the degree to which the discussion is conditioned by the belief that Paul still held at this stage that "the appointed time has grown very short," and that a period of great distress and tribulation lay ahead (I Cor 7:26, 29, 31). Clearly, on these questions Paul was not giving absolute rulings valid for all time and in every situation but, rather, was seeking to give the best advice he could in the particular circumstances which confronted the Corinthians in the mid-50s A.D. The task of Christians today is not simply to quote proof-texts out of context but to seek (as Paul did) the guidance of the Holy Spirit and to apply the basic principles laid down in Scripture to the particular circumstances which they face at the present time.

In his discussion of whether it is right to eat food which has been offered to idols (I Cor 8:1 — 11:1) Paul lays down an important principle: there are practices which may be all right in and of themselves but which should be avoided if they cause offence to those whose conscience is weak. It is not enough for Christians to ask whether something is right for them; they have also to ask what effect their actions may have on others.

Paul is distressed at disturbances which have occurred during worship at Corinth. But God can bring good out of evil: were it not for these disturbances we would never have had Paul's discussion of the Lord's Supper (I Cor 11:17-34), which includes the earliest account of the institution of the sacrament, nor his fine treatment of spiritual gifts (I Cor 12-14). The latter passage is one of those which has a very contemporary ring. Many churches have recently experienced a "charismatic movement." Insofar as such movements stress that every Christian can possess the gifts of the Spirit they are to be warmly commended. Often, conventional Christianity has become too cold and hard and intellectual. The danger, however, is that such movements may go to the opposite extreme and, also, that pride in the possession of certain gifts may lead to division and dissension within congregations. Every believer receives some gift from the Spirit, but it is noticeable that in both of his lists (I Cor 12:8-10 and 12:28-30) Paul places *last* "speaking with tongues," a kind of unintelligible, ecstatic utterance prized by the self-styled "spiritual" Corinthians. Paul will only allow "tongues" if someone "interprets" in understandable speech. Indeed, he prefers a quite different approach and in chapter 14 lays down some guidelines for public worship: worship should build up a congregation in the faith, not divide it; God is to be worshipped not only with the emotions but "with the mind also"; "God is not a God of confusion but of peace." The great thing is to strike the proper *balance* between genuine, Spirit-inspired enthusiasm and doing all things "decently and in order," and to remember that at the top of the list is the greatest gift of the Spirit, *love* (I Cor 13).

In I Cor 15 and again in II Cor 5:1-10, Paul provides a careful treatment of belief in a future resurrection. He still does not actually *describe* the future life but he does explain something of the nature of the resurrection, mainly through illustrations or analogies. Jews could not understand how anyone could live without a body, and Paul teaches the resurrection of the body. But he makes it quite clear that it is not our present physical bodies which survive (hence, there is no need for concern over people killed in car crashes or over cremation); at death God will provide us with a "spiritual body." This is in accordance with Jesus' teaching on the resurrection (see Mark 12:25). A spiritual body will not be subject to pain and decay, and we can be assured that in the future life, the complete personality will survive, an assurance that is not always given by vaguer notions of "the immortality of the soul."

In both I Corinthians (16:1-4) and II Corinthians (chapters 8 and 9), Paul discusses the collection which he organized among his churches for the mother church in Jerusalem, hard-hit by famine and poverty — an early example of "inter-church aid." People today can be moved by news of an earthquake in Mexico or a famine in Ethiopia, but they can also very quickly forget the ongoing crises in the Third World. As Western Christians, we belong to the rich countries which every day get richer while the poor countries get poorer. Paul's discussions in I and II Corinthians challenge us to quit simply *talking* about the needs of the Third World and to put our money where our mouth is — as individuals, as a Church, and as a nation.

Paul also lays down the basic principles of Christian giving. According to some people, "the Church is always asking for money." One might well ask how much such people spend on themselves in the course of even one week! It is all a matter of perspective. Christian giving, says Paul, is to be in response to God's "inexpressible gift"; it is to be in accordance with one's means; and it is to be joyful and of one's own free will since "God loves a cheerful giver." The Macedonian Christians are held up by Paul as the model to follow; their statistics on congregational givings were impressive, but what was even more important, "first they gave *themselves* to the Lord" (II Cor 8:5).

The final, "severe" chapters of II Corinthians (10-13) are of value mainly for the insights they give us into Paul as an apostle and as a human being. In addition to the incredible hardships which Paul endured, "there is the daily pressure upon me of my anxiety for all the churches" (II Cor 11:28). Here we see what it really means to care for others and to "spend and be spent" in their service. Here we see what the Church owes and what Christians even today owe to the apostle Paul.

8. The Letters to the Galatians and the Romans

Have you ever tried to follow Paul's argument in Galatians or to read all the way through Romans? If you have, then you may sympathize with the writer of II Peter who says of the letters written by "our beloved brother Paul" that "there are some things in them *hard to understand.*" He adds the further comment, "... which the ignorant and unstable twist to their own destruction, as they do the other scriptures" (II Peter 3:15, 16). The reference to "the *other* scriptures" shows that this writer already regards Paul's letters as part of Scripture. There is no doubt that Paul was highly regarded in the early Church. It is equally clear that, from the earliest times, people had problems with his letters, since they could be difficult to understand as well as misunderstood and misrepresented.

Nowhere is this mixed verdict on Paul's writings truer than in the case of Galatians and Romans. These two letters take us to the very heart of Paul's thought and, indeed, to the very heart of the Christian message. They have had a decisive influence on later Christian thinkers, particularly Luther, who launched the Protestant Reformation on the basis of the idea of "justification by faith" which he derived from these letters.

A Spirited Defence of the Message

In his other letters Paul deals with a wide range of practical matters but he tends to presuppose the basic message he had preached when founding his churches. In Galatia, however, the very basis of that message had come under attack, so he is forced into a spirited defence of the Gospel. No doubt these attacks compelled Paul to work out his understanding of the Christian message in greater detail and to think through more of its implications. This process also lies behind the writing of Romans. It is the longest letter Paul wrote and is the closest he comes to a systematic discussion of Christian belief (theology) and Christian living (ethics).

There is no denying that these letters are difficult to understand. In Galatians this is partly because the letter was dashed off hurriedly in the heat of controversy. In Romans, particularly, Paul is grappling with some of the most profound and searching questions which humankind has to face. These letters also demonstrate how Paul's message could be misunderstood and misrepresented: that was precisely what had happened in Galatia. A major reason for Paul writing Romans was to explain his version of Christianity to the church at Rome before he arrived there in order to clear up possible misunderstandings in advance. Another major problem was posed by the refusal of most Jews to accept Jesus as the Messiah. How is the Christian community to relate to the ongoing Jewish community? Paul wrestles with and agonizes over this difficult question in Romans 9-11.

The problems will not go away. We need to read these letters and then to re-read them; we need the help of a good commentary or Bible study guide; we need to pray for guidance; and we need the grace of perseverance!

Paul addressed Galatians to a group of churches which he had founded. Paul had just learned that certain people in Galatia were threatening to undo all the good work he did there. "There are some who trouble you and want to pervert the gospel of Christ" by preaching "a gospel contrary to that which we preached to you" (Gal 1:7, 8). Who were these people? Scholars label them the "Judaizers" because they insisted that Gentiles wishing to become Christians had first of all to become converts to Judaism. This meant accepting the whole of the Jewish Law with all its provisions concerning ritual and ceremonial matters (circumcision, Sabbath observance, clean and unclean foods and so on) as well as the moral law.

If this view had prevailed Christianity would never have been anything more than a sect of Judaism. Paul passionately believed that Gentiles could become Christians without first becoming Jews, and he indicates quite clearly that James, Peter and John, the leaders of the Jewish-Christian mother church in Jerusalem, endorsed this view (Gal 2:9). Because this view prevailed, Christianity became a universal religion seeking to share the Good News with people everywhere and accepting people of all nationalities and backgrounds without any preconditions, apart from repentance and faith.

The "Judaizers" not only attacked Paul's message, they attacked Paul himself as being an inferior and unauthorized apostle. Because the validity of his message was so closely bound up with his claim to be an apostle, Paul is forced in the first part of Galatians (1:6 — 2:14) to defend himself. This passage, with its autobiographical details and its glimpses into the history of the early Church, is of special interest.

Galatians poses a number of problems. The Roman province of Galatia included the cities of Antioch in Pisidia, Iconium, Lystra and Derbe where Paul and Barnabas founded churches on the missionary journey described in Acts 13. Some believe that these are the recipients of this letter. On the other hand, Galatia proper lay further north and was probably the region visited by Paul according to Acts 16:6 and 18:23. The geographical location hardly matters except that it ties in with the date of the letter. If Galatians was addressed to the southern cities, it could have been written around A.D. 49, which would make it the earliest letter of Paul and the earliest book of the New Testament. If it was written to the northern region, we would have to place it in the early or mid 50s, probably between Corinthians and Romans. This, in turn, has a bearing on the question of Paul's visits to Jerusalem, in particular, on whether or not the visit described in Gal 2:1-10 is Paul's version of the "Council of Jerusalem" narrated in Acts 15.There has been endless debate but no agreement among scholars on these questions which, fortunately, do not affect our understanding of Paul's message.

On the other hand there is no doubt at all as to when Romans was written. Paul's missionary labours in the eastern portion of the Roman Empire are at an end (Rom 15:19, 23) and his ambition now is to visit Rome itself and then from there to carry the Good News westwards as far as Spain (Rom 15:24). Before he heads for Rome, however, he has one piece of unfinished business: he has to go to Jerusalem along with the delegates from his various churches with the money which has been collected "for the poor among the saints at Jerusalem" (Rom 15:26). This fits exactly the situation at the beginning of Acts 20 where Paul is in Greece (after his long stay in Ephesus) and where the collection delegates are assembling. There are good reasons for thinking that Paul wrote the letter from Corinth.

Salvation as Gift

While we often refer to Paul's "conversion" to Christianity, we tend to forget that before this conversion Paul was not an irreligious person. He was in fact very religious, and as a Jew, he believed in the one God, Creator and Ruler of all things, and accepted the teachings of what Christians call the Old Testament. When Paul became a Christian, however, he acquired two new dominating convictions. *One* was that through the Christ event God in a new way offers salvation as a free gift. The *other* was that this salvation is offered to all.

It is difficult to overemphasize Paul's stress on the grace of God and on salvation as a gift. Paul was doubtless influenced by his own experience. He never forgot how he "persecuted the church of God violently and tried to destroy it" (Gal 1:13). While he was engaged in doing this, God intervened and stopped him in his tracks. Paul could not claim one ounce of credit for becoming a Christian; he owed it completely to the grace of God. He was also convinced that salvation must always be received as a gift by anyone. It is never something which can be earned or merited.

This explains why he took such a strong stand against the Judaizers. They wanted Gentiles to become Jews *before* receiving God's salvation; they wanted Gentiles to observe all the regulations of the Jewish Law as a *precondition*. Paul utterly opposed the idea that there is a whole long list of things people must do *before* God will accept them. No! says Paul. There is nothing anyone must do or can do to earn God's salvation; either it comes as a complete gift or it does not come at all.

No one deserves God's salvation because "all... are under the power of sin" (Rom 3:9). Paul elaborates this insight in the opening chapters of Romans where he gives a penetrating analysis of the human condition. His concern is not with the "sins" which people commit, for they are but symptoms; his concern is with "sin," the underlying disease. At one point Paul traces sin back to Adam, the father of the human race; what Paul is stressing here is the universality of sin and the solidarity of humankind in sin (Rom 5:12-21). He can also speak of humankind being in the grip of evil powers (Gal 4:3, 8; cf. Rom 8:38, 39) and being enslaved in sin (Rom 6:15-23). Principally, he sees sin as disobedience and rebellion against God, people deliberately putting themselves in the centre of things instead of giving that place to God.

Jews know how they ought to live through the commandments given in the Torah, but, Paul charges, they have in fact disobeyed this law (Rom 2:17-29). Gentiles also know the demands of the moral law through conscience, the law written on the heart (Rom 2:14, 15) but they equally have failed to obey it. Hence the verdict, "None is righteous, no, not one" (Rom 3:10). This is a far cry from the popular modern view that people are fundamentally "good at heart." It is far, also, from the view that "virtue is knowledge"; for Paul, the problem is not *knowing* what is good but *doing* it. To some, this view is incredibly pessimistic, but to Paul it is the only realistic position.

The Role of Law

Some of the most difficult passages in the New Testament are those in Galatians and Romans where Paul refers to "law." Part of the problem certainly lies in the fact that Paul uses the word in a number of different senses.

To Jews the law meant the "Torah," the "five books of Moses," Genesis through Deuteronomy. "Torah" in Hebrew means "teaching" or "direction"; much of these books consists of the guidelines God gave the Israelites on how they were to live as God's people. When the Old Testament was translated into Greek, Torah was rendered as *nomos,* which means "law," and which can have a more negative connotation.

Christians have often pictured the Judaism of Paul's day as a legalistic religion in which Jews desperately tried to win God's favour by piling up merit through obedience to the Law. But recent study has shown this is simply untrue.[10] In none of the writings of Palestinian Judaism in this period is law divorced from the idea of the covenant. God in his grace called Israel into a covenant relationship with himself; Torah defines the response of Israel to the grace and goodness of the God of the covenant.

Why then does Paul seem to take such a negative view of law? Why does he emphasize so strongly that people are "not justified by works of the law" (Gal 2:16; cf. Rom 3:28)?

It should be noted that Paul can take a more positive view. The Torah is one of God's gifts to Israel (Rom 9:4). It is holy and just and good (Rom 7:12), and Paul frequently quotes Torah as inspired scripture. From it he cites the story of Abraham who is the great example of faith.

In other contexts Paul stresses that the Law plays a limited role in God's purposes. In Gal 3:24 he says that "the law was our custodian until Christ came." The Greek word used *(paidagōgos)* does not mean "schoolmaster" (*King James Version*). It refers to a slave whom a father would charge with the responsibility of caring for his son, especially escorting him safely to and from school. Paul's thought seems to be that the Law preserved Israel, but also that it prepared the way for the coming of Christ.

In some of the passages where Paul attacks the Law, or more precisely "works of law," it is not Jews he is attacking but Judaizers. What he objects to, as noted above, is imposing the Law on Gentiles as a condition of salvation.

In yet other passages "law" receives a definitely negative evaluation. Here, however, Paul seems to be referring not to Torah, but rather to what we might term "the demands of the moral law thought of apart from God's grace." Law in this sense serves to make us aware of our sinfulness (Rom 3:20). The "Thou shalt nots" of the moral law can even incite people to sin on occasion (Rom 7:5, 7-11). Here Paul is saying that rules in and of themselves cannot make people good; one thing they may do is demonstrate how sinful people really are.

By Grace, through Faith, for Works

Now for the good news, which is what the word "gospel" (Gal 1:6, Rom 1:16) means. Although people do not deserve it, and although they can never earn it, God offers them salvation as a free gift of his grace. God has taken the initiative. God has acted in the person of Christ, especially in his death and resurrection. "God shows his love for us in that while we were yet sinners Christ died for us" (Rom 5:8); "God sent forth his Son... so that we might receive adoption as sons" (Gal 4:4, 5). Paul sets forth this great truth in many ways and one of the commonest is by saying that people are "justified" by God's grace.

For Paul, "justification" means basically God accepting believers into a right relationship with himself. The word has a wide, inclusive significance. In relation to the past it includes the forgiveness of sins; in relation to the present and future it emphasizes that God accepts believers into a new, living, dynamic relationship.

What is the Christian's part in this? Even a gift has to be received, and the gift of salvation is received through *faith*. Faith means people opening themselves so that God can take over and transform their lives. To use an analogy (remembering the limitations of all analogies), I may dive off a pier at Halifax and set out to swim the Atlantic, but there is no way I can accomplish this by my own efforts. But a ship docked at that pier could carry me across the ocean. Trying to swim the Atlantic is like trying to earn salvation. The ship represents God's grace which *can* carry a person across. What one has to do is step on board. This represents faith. Of course, we must take care not to relapse into ideas of earning salvation by saying that Christians are saved *because* of their faith. In a strange way they owe even their faith to God. This is why it can be misleading to speak of "justification by faith." More accurately, what Paul teaches is justification *by* grace, *through* faith.

Paul cites Abraham as the great example of faith. Long before the giving of the Law, Abraham had faith that God would keep his promise and grant him a son although, humanly, this seemed impossible (Gal 3:6-9, Rom 4; see Gen 15:1-6). So,

Paul argues, those with a similar faith in the grace and power of God are the true descendants of Abraham.

By grace, through faith, believers enter into a right relationship with God, "in Christ"; as adopted sons and daughters of God they belong to his family, the Church, and their lives are directed and empowered by the Holy Spirit. For Paul, theology and ethics go hand in hand. Those who have been justified will show in their lives "the fruit of the Spirit" which is "love, joy, peace, patience, kindness, goodness, faithfulness, gentleness, self-control" (Gal 5:22). Chapters 12 through 15 of Romans deal with practical application. "I appeal to you *therefore*... to present your bodies as a living sacrifice..."; because of the whole preceding theological argument, *therefore* this is the way that Christians must live. Paul is *not* unconcerned about "works" in the sense of "Christian living." He commends the Christians at Thessalonica for their "*work* of faith and labour of love" (I Thess 1:3), and he can speak of himself, along with the Christians at Corinth, as "God's fellow *workers*" (I Cor 3:9). Works are not the *root* of salvation, but they must be the *fruit* of salvation. Christians are not saved *by* works, but they are saved *for* works. Paul's complete teaching, therefore, is that salvation or justification is *by* grace, *through* faith, *for* works.

This is virtually the opposite of what many people take Christianity to be: if we live a good life (well, reasonably good), then God will reward us and we can hope to go to heaven when we die. *Paul* does not say, "Do good and you will be saved," but rather, "You have been saved, therefore do good." This is a dynamic doctrine, although it also has its dangers, as Paul himself was aware. In Romans 6 he allows an imaginary objector to ask, "Are we to continue to sin that grace may abound?" If God's grace is everything, then why should Christians not go out on Saturday night and commit all the sins in the book so that God will have all the more chance to forgive them on Sunday morning? Only someone who had completely misunderstood Paul could even ask such a question. Justification entails a complete transformation in a person's life. It is like dying to the old self-centred, sinful ways and beginning a completely new life. "It is no longer I who live, but Christ who lives in me," says Paul (Gal 2:20); Christians are those who are "in Christ Jesus" (Rom 8:1). The Christian is free *from* sin and free *for* a life of joyful and willing obedience to God.

Christians have to be on their guard against a theology of "cheap grace," a Christianity which says, "Hallelujah! I'm saved," but which fails to follow through with the practical application of the Gospel in *every* area of life. They need to grasp Paul's teaching in its fullness — justification ***by*** grace, ***through*** faith, ***for*** works.

9.
The Letters to the Colossians, Philemon, and the Ephesians

In an age in which we are constantly being told that we live in a "global village," in which astronauts have landed on the moon and in which space probes to the planets and beyond have become routine, it is scarcely surprising that many people are asking searching questions about the claims of Christianity. What relevance for the late twentieth century has a faith based on a person who lived nearly 2000 years ago in an obscure corner of the Roman Empire? What contemporary relevance has an organization founded by a dozen or so of this Galilean's followers?

Two major New Testament letters can help us deal with these questions — the Letter to the Colossians (with which the brief note to Philemon is closely associated) and the Letter to the Ephesians. These letters present interpretations of Christ and of the Church which are cosmic in their scope and which speak as convincingly to the twentieth century as they did to the first.

Christ — The Highest Revelation of God

Paul's letter to the church at Colossae was written to one of three cities (the other two were Laodicea and Hierapolis) which lay quite close together in the valley of the river Lycus about 100 miles inland from Ephesus, in the Roman province of Asia (the western part of modern Turkey). Paul himself had not visited Colossae (Col 2:1). The church there had evidently been founded by Epaphras (Col 1:7) as an offshoot of the work directed by Paul in the great city of Ephesus (cf. Acts 19:10, 26). When Paul writes this letter he is in prison (Col 4:18). The commonest view is that the letter was sent from Rome during the imprisonment described at the end of the Book of Acts.

Colossians allows us to see the deep and genuine pastoral concern Paul had even for a congregation which he did not know at first hand. He is profoundly thankful for the reports which have reached him about the Colossians' faith and love (1:3-8), and he assures them that from the day he first heard about the church at Colossae he has not ceased to pray for them (1:9). Yet Paul has also heard disturbing news. At that time the mixing or blending of one religion with another was not uncommon. Evidently, some people in Colossae wanted to combine some elements of the Christian faith with features of other religions to produce a new cult, or a new "mystery" or "philosophy" as they may have termed it. We can catch echoes throughout the letter of this so-called "Colossian heresy," although it is a bit like listening to one end of a telephone conversation: we have to reconstruct the false teaching from what Paul says in attacking it.

The new cult included some Jewish elements (note the mention of circumcision in 2:11 and of "a festival or a new moon or a sabbath" in 2:16). It also borrowed from pagan thought, particularly in the place it gave to "the elemental spirits of the universe" (2:8, 20), the powers behind the planets which were thought to control the lives and destinies of people here on earth — a view still popular among the many modern devotees of astrology! In this system, Christ was given a place probably as one of the angels (2:18) or intermediate beings between God and humankind: however, he would be only one figure among many. The adherents of this cult probably claimed to have had special visions (2:18) and to possess a superior wisdom and knowledge. In practice, their religion was one of rules and regulations with a whole list of "Thou shalt nots" (2:21) in such matters as what food could or could not be eaten.

It was a strange hodge-podge indeed, yet not unlike some of the new sects and cults which have been springing up in North America in recent years. We can be thankful that this threat to the church at Colossae prompted Paul to think through the implications of the Christian faith and to bring these out and explain them in new ways.

Paul was led to stress the uniqueness and the all-sufficiency of God's revelation in Christ. "He is the image of the invisible God" (1:15); it is when believers look at Christ that they see what God is really like. "His is the primacy over all created things" (1:15, *New English Bible*). Paul strains to find words adequate to express how it is through Christ that the entire universe was created (1:16) and continues to be sustained (1:17). There can be no place for other intermediaries or angels or powers: "in him all the fullness of God was pleased to dwell" (1:19, cf. 2:9). In Christ, God has defeated whatever powers threaten the well-being of humanity (2:15) and has reconciled the whole universe to himself. Such a view does not exclude the possibility of truth in other religions and philosophies; it does, however, present Christ as the highest revelation of God. In him "are hid all the treasures of wisdom and knowledge" (2:3). God's revelation in Christ needs to be interpreted and applied by each new generation, but it can never be supplemented or superceded. It is precisely at this point that Christians must part company with Mormons or Christian Scientists or any other group which wants to *add* a new revelation to the one presented in the New Testament.

Breathtaking, also, is Paul's view of the place of the Church in God's plan for us. To "his saints," that is, to Christian believers, God has chosen to reveal the eternal purpose which has now been made known in Christ (1:26, 27). In I Cor 12 and Rom 12 Paul had worked out the idea of the Church as "the body of Christ"; Christians are the members or parts of that body who must co-operate with one another for the sake of the body as a whole. In Colossians the idea is carried a stage further and Christ is seen as "the *head* of the body" (1:18), the brain which directs and controls all the other parts. This emphasizes that the sole allegiance of Christians must be to Christ himself; the Church will fulfil its God-given role only when all its members hold fast to the Head "from whom the whole body, nourished and knit together through its joints and ligaments, grows with a growth that is from God" (2:19).

Human Distinctions Abolished

The short Letter to Philemon was clearly written by Paul at the same time as Colossians and almost certainly to the same destination. In both letters Paul is in prison and is associated with Timothy. Five of the six people who send greetings in Col 4:10-14 also send greetings in Philemon 23, 24. Onesimus, who was sent back to Philemon, evidently travelled with Tychicus, the bearer of the letter to the Colossians (Col 4:7-9). In both letters greetings are sent to Archippus (Col 4:17, Philemon 2). This strongly suggests that the leaders of the house-church addressed in Philemon — Philemon, Apphia and Archippus — must have lived in Colossae. (It has been suggested by some that they actually lived in nearby Laodicea, and that Philemon is therefore the letter to Laodicea referred to in Col 4:16 where instructions are given for the two letters to be exchanged.)

Behind this letter lies an intriguing personal drama. Onesimus, a slave owned by Philemon, had run away, probably stealing some money from his master in the process (see verse 18). He had made his way to Rome, perhaps in much the same way an escaped criminal today might try to lose himself in the big city. But here, in some way unknown to us, Onesimus encountered Paul and was converted to Christianity. Not only that, he became very close to Paul indeed (verses 12, 13). Yet Paul had decided that he must obey the law and return the runaway slave to his master; thus the letter which Paul wrote to Philemon to pave the way for the return of Onesimus.

On the one hand, Paul keeps the law and works within the existing framework of society (cf. I Cor 7:20-24). It would have been madness for Christians at this time to have attempted or even advocated the overthrow of the system of slavery on which the whole economy was based. On the other hand, in sending Onesimus back, Paul not only gives him a testimonial (verses 11-13) and offers to pay back any money he owes (verse 18), but he also introduces a totally new principle into the situation: he appeals to Philemon to take him back "no longer as a slave but more than a slave, as a beloved brother" (verse

16). Here is the practical application of the principle that, in Christ, all human distinctions are abolished. As Paul wrote in Colossians (at almost the same time as he was writing this letter), "There cannot be Greek and Jew, circumcised and uncircumcised, barbarian, Scythian, *slave, free man,* but Christ is all, and in all" (Col 3:11). Here is a principle which in time could reform and revolutionize society from within. We hope that Philemon heeded Paul's advice, although it is interesting to note that Paul did not *demand* obedience. Philemon is treated as a responsible Christian who must make his own decision so that "your goodness might not be by compulsion but of your own free will" (verse 14).

God's "Mysterious" Plan — A New Humanity

For many people the Letter to the Ephesians is one of the great books of the New Testament. Perhaps it is not one of the easiest to understand, but if people are prepared to read and study it, they can come to appreciate the tremendous breadth and depth of its vision and can be helped to draw upon what its writer refers to as "the unsearchable riches of Christ" (Eph 3:8).

There is some kind of a connection between Ephesians and Colossians; about one-third of the words and expressions used in Colossians reappear in Ephesians, although the one letter has certainly not been slavishly copied from the other. Ephesians seems to pick up on many of the thoughts expressed in Colossians (and in some of the earlier letters of Paul) and to take them a stage further. A major difference is that Ephesians is not written to deal with any particular crisis or problem situation in the church. It is couched in more general terms and seems to be the product of further meditation and reflection. Many scholars have noted that it breathes an atmosphere of praise and prayer and have suggested that it may reflect language used in the worship of the Church.

As in Colossians the perspective is a universal one. Christians believe in the God who is the "one God and Father of us all, who is above all and through all and in all" (Eph 4:6). Paul makes the daring claim that the purpose of this God for humankind has been revealed in Christ. Reference is made in 3:9 to "the mystery" of God's plan, but not in the sense of a secret and hidden knowledge such as that which was claimed by some of the mystery religions and cults of the day (and of our day). For Christians the secret of God's purpose is an open secret. In times gone by, people may have been in ignorance as to what God is like, and God's ways may have been hidden from them, but now, in Christ, "the manifold wisdom of God" has been made known to everyone (Eph 3:8-12).

Ephesians, like the rest of the New Testament, does not deny the existence in the universe of powers and forces opposed to God. History appears as a battleground in the struggle between good and evil, between light and darkness. "We are not contending against flesh and blood, but against the principalities, against the powers, against the world rulers of this present darkness, against the spiritual hosts of wickedness in the heavenly places" (Eph 6:12). The Christian is convinced, however, that the decisive battle in this conflict has already been fought and won in the cross and resurrection of Christ. God has exalted Christ to the position of supreme authority in the universe and has "made him sit at his right hand in the heavenly places, far above all rule and authority and power and dominion... and he has put all things under his feet" (Eph 1:20-22). Thus there is no power in all creation which needs to be feared by those who have been "made alive together with Christ" (Eph 2:5) and who own him as Lord.

In this letter the term "church" never refers to a local congregation but always to the one universal Church of Christ. All Christians have the tremendous privilege of being "members of the household of God, built upon the foundation of the apostles and prophets, Christ Jesus himself being the cornerstone" (Eph 2:19, 20). As in Colossians, the Church is the body of which Christ is the Head (Eph 1:22, 23, 4:15, 5:23). Ephesians adds the beautiful picture of the Church as the bride of Christ, comparing the relationship between Christ and the Church to that between husband and wife, a comparison which sheds light on the nature of the Church and on the nature of marriage (Eph 5:21-33).

One of the greatest things which had happened in the early Church was the breaking down of the barrier between Jew and Gentile. Since salvation is purely by God's grace, both Jews and Gentiles — and, indeed, anyone of any race or class or sex —

can come to God and "have access in one Spirit to the Father" (Eph 2:18). God's purpose through the Church is nothing less than to draw all humankind together, to "create in himself one new man" (Eph 2:15), to bring into being a new humanity. An important study of Ephesians by Markus Barth is entitled *The Broken Wall* (referring to Eph 2:14 which says that Christ "has broken down the dividing wall of hostility" between Jews and Gentiles).[11] The world today is divided by Iron and Bamboo Curtains; by walls of jealousy, suspicion, hatred and greed; by political, social, economic and religious barriers. Local Christian congregations must ask themselves if they provide a fellowship in which all barriers are broken down and all may feel equally accepted and at home. All Christians must ask to what extent the Christian Church, fractured by national and denominational divisions, can be seen as the nucleus of a new humanity, offering hope to a divided world.

The Letter to the Ephesians poses a couple of problems. Firstly, there is doubt as to whether it actually was sent to Ephesus. It contains no personal greetings at all, yet Paul spent several years in Ephesus and must have had numerous friends there. Moreover, the reference to Ephesus in the opening greeting (Eph 1:1) is missing in the earliest and best manuscripts. One suggestion, which has a lot to commend it, is that Ephesians was written as a kind of circular letter and that Tychicus (Eph 6:21) was commissioned to take it round a group of churches. If the letter ended up in Ephesus, it is not difficult to understand how the name of that city became attached to the letter.

A second problem is that of authorship. The letter, which claims to be by Paul (Eph 1:1) who is writing from prison (Eph 4:1), had traditionally been classed as one of the "prison epistles" written from Rome. A surprising number of modern scholars, however, have doubted whether Paul was the author of the letter. They point to the considerable number of words not found in any other of Paul's letters and to marked differences in style, a feature confirmed by computer analysis. The thought of the epistle is held by some to be so far beyond that of Paul's other letters that it must be the product of a different writer. The American scholar E. J. Goodspeed suggested that Ephesians is a preface or introduction especially written for the first collected edition of Paul's letters by a disciple and follower of Paul who echoed many of his master's thoughts while also advancing them to a new level.[12] Suggestions for the author have included Onesimus, Timothy, Luke and Tychicus.

Against this viewpoint it can be argued that Paul's thought developed and his vocabulary increased as he dealt with new situations, such as the problem at Colossae, and as he had more leisure in prison to meditate on the implications of faith in Christ. Comparisons of style among Paul's letters may have to reckon with the role of the different scribes used by Paul who may have had some hand in the actual wording of the letters. There are conservative scholars, therefore, who still defend the Pauline authorship of Ephesians, though the majority opinion appears to be against this view. In the final analysis the identity of the human author is not important. The letter is certainly "Pauline" in the sense of summing up and crowning Paul's thought, whether it was written by the apostle himself or one of his disciples. It is important to realize that the inspiration of any book in the Bible is not dependent on any particular theory of authorship.

Guidelines for Christian Living

Concentration on the theological riches of these letters should not make us forget the great stress which Paul always laid on the practical application of Christian beliefs. Paul's discussion of the "Colossian heresy" leads into further discussion of the Christian life, in principle (Col 2:6 — 3:4) and in practice (Col 3:5 — 4:6). Ephesians also has a clear division between the theological discussion in chapters 1 to 3 and the advice on Christian living which occupies chapters 4 to 6.

Reacting no doubt to the more legalistic side of the Colossian cult, Paul emphasizes the transformation which takes place when someone becomes a Christian (Col 2:12, 13). What Christianity produces is not new rules but new people. Ephesians adds an emphasis on the need for development so that Christians may "become mature people, reaching to the very height of Christ's full stature" (Eph 4:13, *Today's English Version*).

Although Christianity is not based on rules and regulations, Paul was well aware of the need to provide guidelines for Christian living. He makes quite clear to the Colossians the kind of life-style with which the believer must have nothing to do (Col 3:5-9) and he does not hesitate to list the chief qualities which mark the life of a Christian, the greatest of which is love "which binds everything together in perfect harmony" (3:14). In both Colossians and Ephesians, more detailed guidelines are set out on the relationships between husbands and wives (Col 3:18, 19; Eph 5:21-33), between parents and children (Col 3:20, 21; Eph 6:1-4) and between masters and slaves (Col 3:22 — 4:1; Eph 6:5-9). Although these resemble to some extent the "tables" of ethical advice given by other writers in the ancient world, they are notable for the repeated reminders that all personal relationships are to be "in the Lord," that is, permeated with the love of Christ. It is the writer's aim that all who read these letters may comprehend "what is the breadth and length and height and depth" and may "know the love of Christ which surpasses knowledge" (Eph 3:18, 19).

10. The Letters to Timothy and Titus

It is no easy task for anyone to be entrusted with the leadership and oversight of a Christian congregation, least of all for a younger minister or priest just starting out and lacking the wisdom that comes from experience. There is no shortage of various "ministers' manuals" on the market which offer all kinds of advice and suggestions on how to be an effective pastor. Three New Testament books which obviously go closely together, two addressed to Timothy and one addressed to Titus, provide very early examples of just such "ministers' manuals." Since they largely consist of advice to young pastors, they are usually referred to as the "Pastoral Epistles," or simply as the "Pastorals."

Timothy and Titus are known to us from Paul's letters as young men who became his personal assistants and who helped him keep in touch with his various churches. In I Timothy it appears that Timothy has been left in charge of the church at Ephesus, while in Titus it is the church in Crete that Titus is to oversee. Both letters picture Paul as an active missionary; in II Timothy, on the other hand, he is a prisoner in Rome and he asks Timothy to join him there.

Who Wrote the Pastorals?

At this point we come up against a whole series of problems which have caused endless discussion and which we might as well meet head on.

Firstly, it is impossible to fit Paul's movements in these letters anywhere into his career as we know it from Acts and from his other letters. It is sometimes held that Paul was released from prison in Rome and undertook further travels during which he wrote I Timothy and Titus, but we cannot be sure of this. In any case, the one or two early references which speak of a release from prison indicate that Paul went, not back east but, rather, westwards to Spain as he was planning to do in Rom 15:24, 28.

Secondly, the picture of the Church which we get in the Pastorals is strangely different from that which comes across in the other letters of Paul. From a letter such as I Corinthians we get an impression of the Church as a vital and dynamic body in which many Christians exercice the varied gifts of the Spirit that have been bestowed upon them; next only to the apostles are the prophets who proclaim God's Word under the inspiration of the Spirit (I Cor 12:28; Eph 4:11). In the Pastorals, however, we miss this Spirit-filled enthusiasm and prophets are not even mentioned. Instead, we seem to be almost at the stage of a hierarchy of clergy — bishops, elders and deacons. Not only that, I Tim 5:17, 18 argues that Church leaders should be paid a regular salary. The Church seems to be much more organized and, indeed, institutionalized than it was in the days of Paul.

Thirdly, there is a somewhat similar difference in the teaching of these letters. Some passages, it is true, do reflect ideas which are characteristic of Paul; "Christ Jesus came into the world to save sinners," we are told in I Tim 1:15, while a text such as Titus 3:5-7 reminds us that salvation is by grace and not by works, for God "saved us, not because of deeds done by us in righteousness, but in virtue of his own mercy... so that we might be justified by his grace...." However, some of Paul's key ideas do not appear here at all, such as his stress on the cross of Christ and on the life of the Spirit. Some of the teaching is expressed in ways quite different from Paul's other letters. Even when the same terminology is used, we have to be on our guard for it may not be used in the same way. For example, the word "faith" is quite frequent in the Pastorals, but in several passages it seems to refer to a body of doctrine which is to be believed and which is also to be carefully guarded so that it can be passed on intact. Thus, in I Timothy 4:6, "the faith" appears to be the equivalent of "the good doctrine." This is quite different from what Paul means by faith, that is, personal trust and commitment through which Christians receive the grace of God and enter into a right relationship with God. All in all, there is a considerable difference in theological atmosphere in the Pastorals: we seem to have left behind the vital, living faith of the earliest Church and to have entered a period where the main concern is with orthodox doctrine.

Fourthly, there is the question of the false teaching which is combatted in these letters. "Certain persons," we are told, "have made shipwreck of their faith" (I Tim 1:19), and careful instructions are given "that you may charge certain persons not to teach any different doctrine, nor to occupy themselves with myths and endless genealogies which promote speculations rather than the divine training..." (I Tim 1:3, 4). What was the nature of these speculations which were threatening the true faith? There can be no doubt that there was a Jewish element in them; reference is made to "the circumcision party" (Titus 1:10) and to "Jewish myths" (Titus 1:14). The emphasis on "speculations" suggests that they claimed to possess a secret revelation, while I Tim 4:3 indicates that they followed a very strict and ascetic life-style, for they "forbid marriage and enjoin abstinence from foods." This adds up to the heresy known as "Gnosticism" which claimed a special knowledge *(gnōsis)* which was hidden from ordinary believers. I Tim 6:20 specifically warns: "Avoid the godless chatter and contradictions of what is falsely called knowledge *(gnōsis)*." While it is not impossible for this kind of false teaching to have existed in Paul's day — it is not unlike the "Colossian heresy" — the closest parallels are to be found in the letters of John and especially in II Peter and Jude which are generally reckoned to be the latest books of the New Testament.

Fifthly, on top of all this, there are marked differences in vocabulary and style between the Pastorals and the letters of Paul. Of the 848 words used in the Pastoral epistles (not counting proper names), 306 are not found elsewhere in Paul's letters. This is a remarkably high percentage. A great many words which are typical of Paul do not occur in the Pastorals. Many turns of phrase and little connecting words, which do not change with a change of subject matter, are used quite differently. Computer analysis has further confirmed the differences in style which are too great to be accounted for by the use of a different secretary (something which may explain less extensive differences in some of Paul's earlier letters).

What does all this evidence add up to? Three views are possible. Firstly, some conservative scholars still hold out for the view that Paul wrote these letters after a release from imprisonment and further missionary work in the eastern Mediterranean. The question which has to be asked here is whether they are not in fact arguing *against* the evidence. Secondly, many modern scholars draw the conclusion that Paul had nothing to do with the Pastorals whatsoever. They are what are termed "pseudonymous" writings, that is, written by an author using someone else's name. This was not at all regarded as a case of forgery and, in fact, it was a common practice in the ancient world. One scholar has recently suggested that Luke wrote the Pastoral Epistles as well as Luke-Acts.

Thirdly, a compromise view is suggested by the fact that while the evidence of a later date is found in the teaching of the letters, they also contain personal references which certainly sound like Paul and which deal with such trivial matters that there would be no point in a later writer making them up (e.g. II Tim 4:9-21; Titus 3:12-15). We know that Paul was a great letter writer and, obviously, he must have written many more letters than the ones we now possess. Some of these would be brief, mainly personal notes, not worth copying and circulating perhaps, but nevertheless preserved and treasured by the recipients. It has been suggested that after the main letters of Paul were collected and published, two or three short notes to Timothy and Titus came to light. Some Church leader of the late first or early second century decided to issue a revised and expanded version of these letters expressing what he sincerely believed would be Paul's message to the changed situation and the new problems of his own day. When you think about it, this kind of thing is common even today. Many college textbooks which have proved to be valuable are revised again and again and may go through fifteen or twenty editions; even when the original author is dead the book is still published in his name, although it has been updated by some younger professor who is now an expert in the field. To take another example, it is still possible to buy a copy of *Mrs. Beaton's Cookery Book* even though the first edition was published back in Victorian times and Mrs. Beaton herself is long dead. The latest edition will tell you how to use a freezer and all kinds of things Mrs. Beaton never heard of. Yet, it is written in the spirit of the original work and with the same basic aim and purpose, and nobody gets up-tight when it is still published in Mrs. Beaton's name. In the same way, then, the Pastoral epistles were written in Paul's name and sought to convey the kind of message Paul would have given to the Church in a later generation.

Nothing is lost by such a view, for we already have ample testimony to Paul's beliefs in his major letters. On the other hand, much is gained for we are given insights into the developing Christian Church at a later period about which we know very little.

Concern for Content

Surveying the problems confronting the Church of his day the author stresses, in particular, the need for sound doctrine, sound organization and sound character.

There are frequent references in the letters to the importance of *sound words* or *sound doctrine*. If you pass these instructions on to believers, the reader is told in I Tim 4:6, "you will be a good minister of Christ Jesus, nourished on the words of the faith and of the good doctrine which you have followed." Christian believers, then as now, often needed help and guidance, especially when they were confronted by faiths and philosophies which claimed to be Christian but actually deviated from the truth of the Gospel. A Christian minister has the education and training which should help to judge such claims and to combat error: "he must hold firm to the sure word as taught, so that he may be able to give instruction in sound doctrine and also to confute those who contradict it" (Titus 1:9).

The writer does not give any extended summary of the content of sound doctrine, though some texts sound like references to an early form of creed, and at two places we seem to have quotations from Christian hymns (I Tim 3:16; II Tim

2:11-13: these are printed in verse form in several modern translations). In these letters the standard of sound doctrine seems to be the teaching of Paul and "the glorious gospel of the blessed God with which I [i.e. Paul] have been entrusted" (I Tim 1:11). Also stressed is the importance of the Scriptures which, at this early stage, would mean the Old Testament seen as fulfilled in Jesus Christ: "All scripture is inspired by God and profitable for teaching, for reproof, for correction, and for training in righteousness..." (II Tim 3:16, 17).

The teaching of the Pastoral letters has often been criticized, and the writer accused, of being concerned with "mere orthodoxy" rather than with a living and vital faith. Yet surely he does have some valid points to make. It is not enough to tell people, "Only believe"; we need also to be concerned with the content of belief. Today, more than ever, Christians find the faith threatened both by direct attacks from without and by subtle deviations from within. Believers need a personal faith in Christ and a commitment to serve him in and through his Church. They also need standards by which to measure what they believe, as well as guidance and help in applying the Church's standards so that they may hold fast to sound teaching "in the faith and love which are in Christ Jesus" (II Tim 1:13).

Structural Considerations: Church Order

Another of the writer's concerns is *sound organization.* In the earliest days of the Church, ministry seems to have been largely "charismatic," that is, anyone who received the gift of the Spirit could preach or teach or pray or whatever. It is not difficult to imagine how such a situation could lead to chaos and to the spread of false teaching. As the original apostles died off and their guiding hand was removed, something more in the way of structure and organization became a necessity. What we see in the Pastorals is a stage in the development of an organized clergy. Three main offices are mentioned: bishops, elders and deacons. Unfortunately the details of the organizational set-up are not spelled out. We have lists of the qualifications required in order to be a bishop (I Tim 3:1-7; Titus 1:7-9), an elder (Titus 1:5, 6) and a deacon (I Tim 3:8-13), but these are character descriptions, not job descriptions! An important role is given to the elder (in Greek, *presbyteros),* an office taken over from Judaism. Churches were probably ruled by a council of elders and I Timothy 4:14 refers to such a group having ordained Timothy (the term used is *presbyterion,* i.e. a "presbytery" or group of elders). We also read of bishops (the basic meaning is "overseers") and, in a passage such as Titus 1:5-9, elders and bishops seem to be virtually equated (cf. Acts 20:17, 28). There are indications, however, that in each congregation one of the elders was taking the lead and acting as bishop/overseer/minister of the church. I Tim 5:17 may indicate a distinction between elders who "rule" a congregation and others who "labour in preaching and teaching." The duties of deacons are less clear but they probably assisted in financial and practical matters and attended to poor relief. Unfortunately, "Church order" has been the cause of endless controversy in later centuries. The Pastorals offer important guidelines, especially in relation to the type of person who should hold office in the Christian Church. They offer a certain corrective to the picture we get of the very earliest Church. But it is much less certain to what extent the pattern of organization which they reveal can be rigidly applied to later and different situations.

A Christian's Personal Qualities

Finally, the Pastorals stress the importance of *sound character.* There are frequent references to the various qualities which ought to characterize the lives of believers. Scholars point out that many of these (piety, godliness, purity and so on) represent the ideals which were propounded by the best ancient pagan writers. There is nothing wrong with that: Christians certainly share the aims and ideals of good people of all ages. What is different in the case of Christians is the motivation and power for ethical living. If Christians are exhorted to "be careful to apply themselves to good deeds," this is in the context of a reminder of how "God saved us" by his grace and gave us "the Holy Spirit which he poured out upon us richly through Jesus Christ our Saviour" (Titus 3:5-8).

11. The Gospel According to Mark

For long centuries Mark's Gospel was neglected and considered to be by far the least important of the four. About nine-tenths of its material is found in Matthew (about half of it is also found in Luke). The traditional view saw it as merely an abbreviation of Matthew. Almost all modern scholars now believe it was really the other way round: Mark's Gospel was written first, and Matthew and Luke both drew upon it as one of their sources. It is a case of "the last shall be first." Today, Mark is considered to be particularly important because it was the first Gospel written and because it was a model which others followed.

The Gospel itself gives no direct clue as to how and when it was written. Nonetheless, most scholars are prepared to acknowledge that there is probably considerable truth in the tradition handed on by the early second century Christian writer Papias[13] and the later second century writer Irenaeus.[14] They claim that the Gospel was written in Rome, after the death of the apostles Peter and Paul, by someone called Mark, who had been the "interpreter" for Peter. These claims are modest and have the ring of truth about them. Papias acknowledges that the writer was not himself an eyewitness and that the Gospel is not "an ordered exposition," that is, the events are not necessarily recorded in the correct chronological order. The Gospel itself seems to fit well into the situation suggested by this tradition: Jewish terms and customs are explained for the reader; there is a strong interest in Gentile missions; the stress on the cost of discipleship fits the period following the terrible persecution under Nero in A.D. 64 in which Peter and Paul were martyred; and the air of crisis in the Gospel fits this period of world-shaking events, including the great Jewish rebellion which broke out in A.D. 66 and which culminated in the fall of Jerusalem and the destruction of the Temple in A.D. 70. Although arguments have been advanced for both Galilee and Syria as the place of writing, most scholars would support the view that the Gospel was written around A.D. 65-70, in Rome, for the predominantly Gentile Christian church there.

Later tradition identified the "Mark" mentioned by Papias and Irenaeus with the "John Mark" who appears in Acts 12:12, 12:25, 13:5, 13:13, 15:37 as the cousin of Barnabas and companion of Paul on his journey to Cyprus, and who is mentioned by Paul in Colossians 4:10, Philemon 24 and II Timothy 4:11, and with "my son Mark" who is referred to in I Peter 5:13.

Mark's Sources

Granted that the Gospel was written in Rome about A.D. 65-70, where did the author get his source material from? Probably he drew on traditions preserved by the Christian congregation in Rome, at least some of which would already be in written form. Scholars detect indications that he used earlier collections of the sayings of Jesus and also believe that units like chapter 13 may have circulated earlier as separate tracts. The passion narrative (chapters 14 and 15) must surely have already been put together as a connected account. Special interest attaches to the claim of Papias that Mark wrote down what he could remember of *Peter's* account of the sayings and doings of Christ. Peter is mentioned twenty-six times in the Gospel, and there is a considerable amount of material which could well have originally come from Peter.

Even though the Gospel was written in Rome, it is quite likely that at an earlier stage much of the material used by Mark had come from Galilee. Although Jesus was almost certainly in Jerusalem several times in the course of his ministry, Mark's Gospel places most of Jesus' ministry, apart from the last week of his life, in Galilee. The Gospel shows a special interest in Capernaum which was an important early Christian centre. It may well be that the traditions which found their way to Rome were earlier collected and passed on by the church at Capernaum. A flood of new light has been shed on this by excavations at Capernaum which have uncovered the remains of the house of Peter which served as a place of Christian worship and pilgrimage before the end of the first century.[15] This must be "the house" mentioned in Mark 1:29 (cf. also 1:33, 2:1). Galilean Christians would naturally remember and record aspects of Jesus' ministry in Galilee, including events in which Peter played a prominent role.

Discussion of the sources and writing of Mark's Gospel inevitably involves guesswork and speculation. What we do know directly is the finished Gospel which he produced. Recent studies of Mark's "redaction" or editing of the work and of its literary style have highlighted some of the more important features of the earliest Gospel.

A Sense of Urgency

Any reader must surely be impressed with the urgency of the message which Mark spells out. The Gospel is not long (it can easily be read in one sitting — try it sometime), and it is mostly made up of quite short units so that the scene keeps changing and the pace seldom slackens. Jesus moves from one location to another more than forty times in the Gospel. Mark would not have won a prize in a contest for Greek literature, but his language is forceful and direct. For example, he is very fond of the Greek word which means "immediately"; it occurs eleven times in chapter 1 alone! Every now and again Mark slips into using the present tense: "And they *come* bringing to him a paralytic... and seeing their faith Jesus *says* to the paralytic..." (2:3, 5). Though not very correct grammatically, it does tend to make the stories more vivid.

This same note of urgency is carried over into the portrait of Jesus himself. Mark gives some of Jesus' teaching, but not a great deal. For him, Jesus is not so much a wise religious teacher as a man of action, the one through whom the Kingdom of God is breaking into history, the one in whom the power of God is at work, the one who leads the battle against the forces of Satan.

References to the time of the end and the Day of Judgment, especially in chapter 13, also make Mark's message more urgent. It has often been alleged that Mark (and Jesus, too) expected the end of the world to come very soon. Since that did not happen it might appear that they were both wrong. But a careful reading of chapter 13 (especially verses 32-37) shows that, according to Mark at least, Jesus did not teach that the end will come *immediately,* but that it will come *suddenly.* What he emphasized was the need for constant watchfulness: live every day as if it were your last.

Mark's urgent message challenges the reader to decide for or against Jesus Christ. This is a life-or-death decision. The author would surely be mystified by the lukewarm, nominal Christianity that characterizes so many professing Christians today; he would clearly agree with the phrase, "the nonsense of neutrality."

Jesus' Authority Emphasized

Another feature of Mark's presentation is the emphasis on the authority of Jesus. The figure of Christ completely dominates the Gospel. It is often said that Mark gives the most human portrait of Jesus. There is some truth in this view. He does not hesitate to depict Jesus showing a wide range of human emotions (see 3:5, 8:12, 14:33) where the other Gospels are generally more guarded. It is also true that Mark, in particular, is reticent in depicting Jesus making explicit claims for himself during his ministry. In fact, a characteristic of Mark's portrait of Jesus is what has been called "the messianic secret." While Jesus is designated "Son of God" by a heavenly voice at the Baptism (1:11) and at the Transfiguration (9:7) and is recognized as such by demons (1:24, 3:11), he frequently commands people to keep quiet about his divine status and God-given powers (see e.g. 1:44, 5:43, 8:30, 9:9). Only at the end of his life, during the trial before the high priest, does he openly admit to being "the Messiah, the Son of the Blessed [i.e. God]" (14:61, 62). Recently, some scholars have suggested that Mark had in mind Christians who thought of Jesus too much in terms simply of a divine wonder-worker; he sought to counterbalance such an emphasis by stressing the paradox that Jesus was also the Son of man who must suffer and die.

Yet there can be no doubt whatsoever that Mark himself believed Jesus to be both Messiah and Son of God. He shows us the power of God working in a unique way in Jesus' ministry. Through Jesus, God reveals his will, forgives sin, defeats the powers of evil, heals disease and demands unqualified obedience. "He taught them as one who had authority, and not as the scribes" (1:22). Television programs often feature interviews with people who are said to be "authorities" on various subjects. For most viewers, whether such people possess a Ph.D. or some high-sounding title is neither here nor there. By the way the persons speak and behave and answer questions, it is very quickly apparent whether or not they really are an "authority." Jesus, as Mark depicts him, is above all an authoritative figure. Mark all along invites his readers to find in Christ the one through whom God speaks to them, defeats the powers which threaten them, heals them and demands their obedience.

Be Prepared to Count the Cost

If Mark challenges his readers to commit themselves to this authoritative figure, he leaves them under no illusion about *the cost of discipleship.* This theme runs right through the Gospel but is especially evident in the section on Jesus' journey to Jerusalem which extends from 8:31 to 10:52. This section breaks down into three sub-sections (8:31 — 9:29, 9:30 — 10:31, 10:32 — 52): each begins with a solemn prediction of Jesus' suffering and death, and stresses that Christian believers must be prepared to deny themselves, take up their cross and follow Christ.

Norman Perrin has pointed out an interesting parallel which runs through the Gospel.[16] We are told that John the Baptist *preached* (1:7) and that he was then *delivered up* (1:14). Jesus also came *preaching* (1:14) and he, too, was "*delivered* into the hands of men" (9:31; also see 10:33). Finally, it is made clear that Christians, too, must *preach* the gospel (13:10) and also expect to be *delivered up* (13:9, 11). In a hostile world the true proclamation of the Gospel is bound to provoke opposition.

It is often said that the Church today tends to be met with apathy rather than with opposition; perhaps that says something about our preaching of the Gospel. Certainly, as the idea declines that the West is "officially" Christian, and as committed Christians become more obviously a minority, Mark's message will become more and more relevant to the contemporary situation. Every true believer must be prepared to count the cost.

Witnessing to the Lord

One other feature of Mark deserving special mention is his interest in the spread of the Good News. It seems likely that the original end of Mark is missing. The oldest manuscripts stop at 16:8 in what seems to be the middle of the empty tomb story: verses 9-20 were apparently added later in an attempt to bring the book to a more satisfactory conclusion. We have no way of knowing, therefore, if Mark originally concluded with a command to go and make disciples of all nations (like the "Great Commission" with which Matthew closes). But, long before the end of the Gospel, Mark impresses on his readers the importance of sharing the Good News with others. He notes that Jesus ventured into Gentile areas such as Tyre and Sidon and the Decapolis. He quotes sayings about the Gospel being preached "to all nations" (13:10) and "in the whole world" (14:9). If Mark was indeed written originally for Christians in the city of Rome, how significant it must have been for them to read that it was a Roman centurion who, when he witnessed Jesus' death on the cross, exclaimed, "Truly this man was the son of God" (15:39).

We must remember that Christians in Rome around A.D. 65-70 were a small, persecuted minority in no position to launch an expensive, highly-organized program of missionary outreach. In fact, it is much more likely that Christians could only witness among their own family, friends and place of work. How appropriate to their situation (and to that of many people today) is the conclusion of the story of the healing of the Gerasene demoniac in 5:1-20. After the man had been healed he asked permission to follow Jesus as he went on to another district. Jesus refused this request and instead told the man, "Go home to your friends, and tell them how much the Lord has done for you, and how he has had mercy on you." So the man was left in his own neighbourhood and among his own people and there he "began to proclaim... how much Jesus had done for him." The Roman Christians were not to withdraw from the difficult situation in which they found themselves but were to witness to their Lord *in* that situation. Mark's Gospel still challenges Christians today to respond to the urgent message of the authoritative Christ and faithfully and fearlessly to witness to the Good News in whatever situation God has placed them.

12. The Gospel According to Matthew

Matthew was long considered the first of the Gospels to be written and the most important of the four. It is still highly valued, especially for its record of the teaching of Jesus. When we think of Jesus' teaching we think automatically of the Sermon on the Mount and this, of course, is found in Matthew (chapters 5, 6, 7).

To be honest, we have to admit that the origins of this Gospel are somewhat obscure. The work itself gives us no indication of how it came to be written. The only scrap of information which may be relevant comes to us from the early second century writer Papias who says, "So then Matthew recorded the sayings *(logia)* in the Hebrew tongue, and each interpreted them to the best of his ability."[17] Later Christian writers took this to refer to the first Gospel, and before long it was accepted that the apostle Matthew had written it in Hebrew (or Aramaic) and then translated it into Greek. This view was for a long time the only one Roman Catholics were allowed to hold and it is still the view held by many conservatives to this day.

Modern scholars recognize several difficulties in the traditional view. The *logia* or "sayings" mentioned might possibly refer to the first Gospel (although it of course contains more than the sayings of Jesus). Our Matthew, however, was *not* translated from Hebrew or Aramaic. The great majority of scholars recognize that it was written in Greek. They also hold that it used Mark's Gospel (also in Greek) as one of its main sources. This makes it difficult to think of the apostle Matthew as the author; if he had written it, surely he would have been able to draw directly on his own memories of Jesus' ministry rather than rely so heavily on Mark's outline of events. It is clear that the man who composed Matthew's Gospel was (like Mark and Luke) basically an editor or compiler who put together material drawn from earlier sources.

It seems unlikely, therefore, that Papias' *logia* refer to the first Gospel. Some scholars suggest, however, that Papias may have been referring to one of the sources now embodied in the Gospel. There are two possibilities here. 1) The Gospel appears to have drawn on a collection of the sayings of Jesus to which Luke also has access. This collection could have been written down at quite an early stage. What is more, there is evidence that these sayings were originally in Aramaic. This would fit the *logia* of Papias perfectly; it may well be that this collection of sayings was credited to the apostle Matthew. 2) There is another possibility, based on the fact that *logia* could mean "oracles," that is, Old Testament prophecies or proof-texts (the word is used in this sense in Romans 3:2). One of the characteristic features of Matthew's Gospel is its quotation of a whole series of Old Testament texts fulfilled in the life of Christ. If this collection of proof-texts originally existed independently, it could have been the *logia* ascribed to the apostle Matthew.

If either of these possibilities is right, and if the name of Matthew was associated with one of the sources of the Gospel, it is not too difficult to see how in time it would come to be attached to the Gospel as a whole.

As far as the final compiler of the Gospel is concerned, he was content to remain anonymous and we have to accept this fact. For the sake of convenience, however, we will continue to refer to the author as "Matthew."

If Mark's Gospel was written about A.D. 65-70, and if we allow time for it to be copied and to circulate among Christian churches, to come to the attention of Matthew, and then to be used by him as one of his sources, it is difficult to date Matthew much before A.D. 80. Scholars like to guess where Matthew may have been written. The best guess is probably the great city of Antioch in Syria which was an important early Christian centre.

Matthew is often referred to as the Jewish-Christian Gospel. Many of the traditions incorporated in the Gospel may have been passed down in an early Jewish-Christian community. There are frequent references to Jewish beliefs and customs. The Gospel speaks not of "the Kingdom of God" (as in Mark) but of "the Kingdom of Heaven"; this means exactly the same thing, but reflects the Jewish reluctance to mention God, the word "heaven" being used as a substitute.

In its final form, however, the Gospel fully supports the mission to the Gentiles. Indeed it is in the closing verses of Matthew that we find Christ's great missionary command, "Go therefore and making disciples of all nations..." (see Matt 28:18-20). Moreover, as recent studies have shown, Matthew appears to come from the period around A.D. 80 to 90 when church and synagogue, Christianity and Judaism definitely and finally parted company. This helps explain why Matthew is also the most *anti*-Jewish of the Gospels. Chapter 23 with its long list of "woes" directed against the "scribes and Pharisees, hypocrites" probably reflects not just the conflicts of Jesus' day but the tension between Matthew's Christian community and the local Jewish synagogue. We see here, unfortunately, the beginnings of the long, unhappy history of Jewish-Christian conflict.

Educating Adult Christians

Matthew's Gospel places great emphasis on teaching, or as we would say today, Christian education. In Matthew's situation this would mean primarily *adult* Christian education — the education of converts preparing for baptism and the continuing education of members of Christian congregations.

If Mark presents Jesus primarily as a man of action, Matthew, with greater resources at his disposal, concentrates mainly on presenting Jesus as the great Teacher, the one who has brought the final and authoritative fulfilment of the Law of the Old Testament. In the Gospel the only person who teaches is Jesus himself; the disciples are there to listen and learn. At the very end of the Gospel, however, they are commanded to go and make disciples of all nations, "*teaching* them to observe all that I have commanded you" (28:20). To the Church is given the task of carrying Jesus' teaching to all people.

It is highly probable that Matthew himself was a teacher. Like a good teacher, he arranges his material systematically and by topics to make it easier for his students to understand, study and learn. Scholars have recognized that Matthew has re-arranged the material at his disposal so as to form five great blocks of Jesus' teaching grouped according to subject matter. These blocks can be classified as follows:

1) The Sermon on the Mount (chapters 5, 6, 7)
2) The Mission Charge (chapter 10)
3) Parables of the Kingdom (13:1-52)
4) The Life of the Church (chapter 18)
5) The End of the Age (chapters 23, 24, 25).

Each block is rounded off with a similar phrase such as, "And when Jesus finished these sayings..." (7:28; cf. 11:1, 13:53, 19:1, 26:1).

These five blocks of teaching more or less alternate with five sections of narrative (dealing with the events of Jesus' ministry) and these take up the greater part of the Gospel. They are preceded by the stories of Jesus' birth and infancy in chapters 1 and 2 and followed by the accounts of his death and resurrection in chapters 26, 27 and 28.

It is probably no accident that Matthew provides *five* blocks of teaching. We recall that there are five books in the Law (Genesis through Deuteronomy) and Matthew seems to be indicating that Jesus' teaching parallels and fulfills the Law. Jesus is a new but greater Moses who gives his teaching on a mountain (5:1) just as Moses delivered the Law to Israel at Mount Sinai.

In a day when even many in the churches apparently think that Christian education is only for the under-10s, Christians could well recall Matthew's concern with adult and continuing education. In an age of controversy over which curriculum to use, it is instructive to turn back to the first Christian education curriculum ever produced — Matthew's Gospel.

Stressing Continuity

All four Gospels present the life of Jesus as a *fulfilment of the Old Testament,* but Matthew is the one who has the greatest interest in this subject. At the very outset he shows how Jesus is the son of Abraham and also the son of David, thus qualifying him as the expected Messiah (1:1-17).

In particular, Matthew draws our attention to a whole series of Old Testament passages which he links with events in the life of Jesus. In each case the quotation is introduced with a similar formula such as, "All this took place to fulfil what the Lord had spoken by the prophet..." (1:22). Some scholars have suggested that these Old Testament prophecies or testimonies originally existed as a separate pamphlet or "Book of Testimonies." It does seem likely that one of the things the very earliest Christians did was to go through the Old Testament picking out passages which they now saw in a new light and which they connected with events in Jesus' life. It may well be, therefore, that Matthew was able to draw on such a collection and work the material into his Gospel at the appropriate points.

This kind of use of Old Testament texts has frequently been criticized. It has been alleged that the passages quoted have been twisted out of their original meaning. Careful examination, however, usually shows that Matthew remains true to the broader context of the original passage and that he is saying something meaningful and, indeed, profound about the Christ event. For example, in 2:15, in connection with the flight to Egypt, Hosea 11:1 is quoted: "Out of Egypt have I called my son." Of course, when Hosea said this he was referring to the Israelites (God is the Father, the people are his "son") who went down into Egypt and whom God rescued at the time of the Exodus and led out into the desert to serve and follow him. The Hosea passage goes on to remind us how miserably the Israelites failed the God who loved them. Matthew sees a significant parallel between the experience of the Israelites and that of Jesus. Like them, Jesus was delivered from danger through God's providence and, like them, Jesus was called to serve God. In a sense Jesus represents the people of God. He is what God's people were meant to be, but failed to be. God delivered him, like Israel, but with this difference — Jesus went on to live a life of perfect obedience to God. Israel is spoken of as "son" of

God in the Old Testament, but Jesus is *the* Son of God in the New Testament.

Some early Christians were tempted to throw away the Old Testament, and some modern liberals contrast the God of the Old Testament, a God of wrath, with the God of the New Testament, a God of love. The very first book (indeed, the very first chapter) of the New Testament warns us that it is quite wrong to do this. The Old and New Testaments belong together for both present the dynamic, ongoing story of God's plan of salvation, beginning with Israel and culminating in the sending of Jesus the Christ, the son of David and the son of Abraham.

The Church — A Central Motif

Matthew has always been recognized as the Gospel which emphasizes *the Church.* It might almost seem as though he was writing for the benefit of many people today who say, "I can be a Christian without belonging to the Church." For one thing, Matthew traces *the founding of the Church* back to Jesus himself. Only Matthew quotes Jesus' saying, "You are Peter, and on this rock I will build my church" (16:18). More important than this, in chapters 14 through 17 especially, we are shown Jesus at work with his disciples, teaching them and training them and testing them so that they can form the nucleus and the leadership of a new people of God after his death.

Matthew even shows some concern about *the structure of the Church.* In 18:15-17 he provides us with a four-stage procedure to follow when a member of the Church sins against a fellow-Christian. If this reads a bit like a church manual, then perhaps it is important to note that the teaching which immediately follows (18:21-35) deals with the importance of forgiveness. The whole concern of the procedure is not to expel someone from the Church, but to enlist the help of the whole congregation in bringing about a reconciliation. The Church needs to have some rules and some structures, but these should not conflict with the aim of dealing with people in a truly Christian spirit.

The *task of the Church* is clearly spelled out by Matthew in the Great Commission of 28:18-20 ("Go therefore and make disciples of all nations...") and again in the Mission Charge of chapter 10 where we hear the living Christ giving the Church of Matthew's day (and, indeed, the Church of our day) its marching orders.

This Gospel might well suggest that there is "no salvation outside the Church." But it does not state that mere membership in the Church guarantees salvation because of the theme of *the judgment of the Church* to which the Gospel so frequently alludes. For example, the explanation of the parable of the wheat and the tares, which is found only in Matthew (13:36-43), stresses the mixed nature of the Church at the present time, and teaches that, at the Judgment, the Church will be purged of all that is wrong and unworthy.

Do unto Others...

If one word could sum up Matthew's understanding of the Christian life, it would have to be *righteousness*. For him, "righteousness" is the way of life taught and practised by Jesus and it is now to be the way of life of the Christian community. The demands are high: the Christian must do not less, but more, than the scribes and Pharisees who keep all the details of the Law (5:20). We must hunger and thirst for righteousness (5:6). Matthew's Gospel passes on to us one of the most down-to-earth definitions of who the "righteous" are: they are those who feed the hungry, give a drink to the thirsty, welcome the stranger, clothe the naked and visit the sick and those in prison (25:31-46).

Matthew's outlook resembles that of the letter of James. He would heartily agree that faith without works is dead (see James 2:14-26). But do not think that Matthew's Gospel expects Christians to follow the demanding way of righteousness in their own strength. Before we do anything, God has already acted by sending Jesus as the promised Messiah (1:1, 17) who "will save his people from their sins" (1:21). Even Paul, with all his tremendous stress on sinful humans' inability to earn God's salvation by their own efforts, ends up telling Christians who have responded to the Gospel in faith, "Bear one another's burdens, and so fulfil the law of Christ" (Gal 6:2). There is "a law of Christ" which must guide the day to day living of committed Christians. Paul on the one hand, and Matthew and James on the other, certainly differ in their emphasis but (contrary to what some scholars maintain) they do not really contradict one another.

Despite the fact that most of Mark is incorporated into Matthew, and that there is overlapping with Luke as well, we still find much of value that is only in Matthew. Moreover, the author has restructured all his material so as to provide his own quite distinctive portrait of Jesus, a portrait for which we should never cease to be grateful.

13. The Gospel According to Luke

In a number of ways Luke's Gospel stands apart from the other three. For one thing it is clear that it was originally Part I of a two-volume work on "The Origins of Christianity," with what we now call the Acts of the Apostles constituting Part II. A comparison of the introduction to Acts (Acts 1:1, 2) with the preface to the Gospel (Luke 1:1-4) shows that Luke is "the first book," dealing with "all that Jesus began to do and teach," while Acts is a continuation of the same story, recounting how Jesus continued to act in and through the early Church. When the books of the New Testament were being put together Luke was separated from the second volume, classified as a "Gospel" and placed along with the other three Gospels. In many ways this was an unfortunate separation and modern scholars do us a service when they speak of "Luke-Acts" (with a hyphen) and remind us that these two books were originally a unity with many of their key themes running through both volumes.

More so than the other Gospel writers Luke sees himself as an historian; Luke-Acts is, in fact, the first Christian history. Luke writes in better, more literary Greek than most of the other New Testament writers and in his preface (Luke 1:1-4) he indicates that he has followed the method of all good historians, ancient or modern. He himself was not an eye-witness of the events he records but over a period of time he has sought out reliable sources of information. Evidently, there was no lack of material: already "many have undertaken to compile a narrative of the things which have been accomplished among us." Utilizing these sources the author seeks to draw up as comprehensive, accurate and orderly an account as possible. Of course, like the other Gospel writers, Luke is a theologian as well as an historian. He selects and presents his material in order to convey his view of the Christian faith and of the Christian Church.

Luke dedicates his work to "most excellent Theophilus" so that he "may know the truth concerning the things of which you have been informed." Unfortunately, we know nothing at all about Theophilus apart from this brief reference. "Most excellent" was the usual way of addressing a Roman governor (see Acts 23:26, 24:2, 26:25) and there is something to be said for the view that Luke-Acts is the first Christian "apology" or defence, written to show a Roman official, who had only incomplete information, that Christianity was not a subversive movement and that it was possible to be a good Christian and a good Roman citizen at the same time.

The author of Luke-Acts was content to remain anonymous. It is not until the late second century that Christian tradition identifies him as "Luke, the follower of Paul" and "Luke, the physician,"[18] the Luke who is mentioned three times in the New Testament, though only in passing (Philem 24; Col 4:14; II Tim 4:11). Most scholars accept Luke as the author; since he is a very minor New Testament character and not one of the apostles it is difficult to see why anyone would invent the idea that he wrote the Gospel and Acts. Colossians 4:14 lists Luke among a group of Gentile Christians and there is much in Luke-Acts to support the idea that he was a Gentile (probably the only non-Jew among the writers of the New Testament). Paul also refers to him as "the beloved physician." The argument of some earlier scholars that Luke's authorship could be proved by the use of technical medical terms in the Gospel has now been abandoned; the language is not any more medical than that of most ancient writers. Nonetheless, there is nothing in the Gospel inconsistent with its having been written by a doctor.

A careful study of Luke's Gospel suggests what some of the author's sources were. Most scholars agree that Mark's Gospel was one of them; Luke used about half of Mark's material and also took over his general outline of events. He seems to have drawn on an early collection of Jesus' sayings to which Matthew also had access. In addition to these sources he used material not found in any other Gospel, including many well-loved passages ranging from the Christmas story of the shepherds to the parables of the Good Samaritan and the Prodigal Son. The author probably gathered at least some of his source material in Palestine and possibly drew on traditions preserved by churches in such places as Jerusalem and Caesarea.

Like any historian, Luke had to be selective in using the materials at his disposal. The fact that he used only half of Mark's Gospel shows clearly that he was not able to include everything. Naturally, it is in what he decided to include and in what he decided to leave out that we can best discern his personal convictions and his own characteristic understanding of the Christian Gospel. Luke is today viewed as much more than a mere collector of facts and compiler of sources. Most recent studies show an ever-growing respect for him as a literary artist, historian and theologian. Especially since the publication in 1954 of an influential book by the German scholar, Hans Conzelmann,[19] it has been widely recognized that Luke was one of the first Christians to see how the life of Jesus relates to the whole sweep of human history and especially to "salvation history," God's dealing with his own chosen people throughout the centuries.

God's Action in History

Luke sees history divided into three great periods which we could label (1) The Time of Israel, (2) The Life of Jesus and (3) The Time of the Church.

Period (1), The Time of Israel, covers the Old Testament but goes up to and includes John the Baptist as the last great representative of the Old Testament order; this is the time of prophecy and preparation. Gentile he may be, but Luke is thoroughly familiar with both the contents and the language of the Old Testament (though he has read it not in the original Hebrew but in Greek translation).

Period (2), The Life of Jesus, represents God's decisive intervention in human history for our salvation. Following in the main Mark's outline, Luke subdivides this period into three sections: Jesus' ministry in Galilee (Luke 4:14 — 9:50), Jesus' journey to Jerusalem (Luke 9:51 — 19:27) and Jesus in Jerusalem (19:28 — 24).

Luke's really original contribution is his emphasis on period (3), The Time of the Church. Luke was the only Gospel writer to continue his work with a history of the early Church. Some early Christians expected the end of the world to come soon. Luke does not cut out all references to "the end," but his selection of passages from Mark indicates that he definitely plays down the idea and does not believe that the end is going to come soon. Not only is he able to look *back* over the first period of Christian history, but what is even more significant, he is able to look *forward* and recognize that history is going to continue and that there are going to be future generations of Christians who will read his two-volume history. (Individuals would not write history books if they thought the world was going to end tomorrow!).

Luke sees how God has acted, and is still active, in history. Salvation history, moreover, is directly related to world history (and world geography). In Luke 1:5, 2:1, 2 and 3:1, 2, Luke links the life of Jesus to clearly dateable persons and events in the history of the Roman Empire. The Gospel both opens and closes in the great city of Jerusalem, the one Jewish city of which everyone in the Empire would have heard. What Luke is telling us here is that "this was not done in a corner" (see Acts 26:26).

For those who lay all the stress on personal decision and a very individualistic and subjective kind of Christian faith, Luke's emphasis on "salvation history" is not all that appealing. Luke, however, presents a tremendous vision of the working out of God's purposes in history, a vision which can inspire Christians even in this day and age when it is so often the Marxists and Communists who believe that history is on their side. He sees the continuity of God's work in history — beginning away back in Old Testament times, coming to a climax in the life of Christ but also continuing through his own day and beyond. Christians today are privileged to belong to the Time of the Church: they have a part in the continuing story of the people of God whose first apostles, saints and martyrs are portrayed by Luke for the instruction and inspiration of later generations.

Christ's Universal Significance — Outreach

While Luke deals with the third period of salvation history (The Time of the Church) mainly in the Book of Acts, even in his Gospel he has in mind the way in which Christianity, after Jesus' death and resurrection, is going to launch out into a great, world-wide movement. In Acts he will tell how Christianity began as a Jewish movement, then spread to the Samaritans and finally accepted Gentile converts. Correspondingly, in the Gospel, while Jesus deals mainly with Jews, Luke also stresses his dealings with Samaritans and Gentiles. Three passages found only in Luke illustrate Jesus' surprisingly favourable attitude to the Samaritans who were considered by most Jews to be half-breeds and heretics: the account of Jesus in Samaria (Luke 9:51-56), the parable of the Good Samaritan (Luke 10:25-37) and the story of the Thankful Samaritan (Luke 17:11-19) Similarly Luke finds ways of bringing out the universal significance of Christ even in his Gospel: he traces Jesus' descent, for example, not just from Abraham the father of the Jews but from Adam, the first human (Luke 3:38). In his account of John the Baptist he copies Mark in quoting the Isaiah passage about the "voice of one crying in the wilderness," but he continues the quotation on for a further two verses so that he can end with the line, "and all flesh shall see the salvation of God" (Luke 3:4-6; cf. Mark 1:2, 3, Isaiah 40:3-5). And only Luke recounts, in addition to a mission of the Twelve, a mission of the Seventy (Luke 10:1-20) which clearly has symbolic significance since the Jews believed that there were seventy Gentile nations in the world.

A Thirst for Justice

There is a sense in which Luke's interests are practical rather than theological. He is not interested in a theory of the atonement. He leaves out the two main texts in Mark's Gospel which hint at the meaning of Jesus' death, one which interprets it in terms of "a ransom for many" (Mark 10:45), and the other which interprets it in terms of the "blood of the covenant" (Mark 14:24). Luke sees the life of Jesus, rather, as a drama which moves inevitably towards its tragic climax, the hour which belongs to the power of darkness (Luke 22:53). Then with the Resurrection, the Ascension and the giving of the Holy Spirit, the verdict on Christ's life is dramatically reversed and tragedy is turned into triumph.

Luke's interest in social action has often been noted. Only he adds to the account of John the Baptist's preaching the practical advice which John gave to the crowds, to tax collectors and to soldiers on how their religion should be applied in their daily lives (Luke 3:10-14). Luke's sympathy for the poor is evident: he records the first beatitude as simply, "Blessed are you poor" (Luke 6:20; Matt 5:3 refers to "the poor in spirit") and he adds "woes" to those who are rich and those who are "full now" (Luke 6:24, 25).

One of the most contemporary features of Luke's Gospel is his concern for the status of women. It is to Luke that we owe most of our information on Mary and Elizabeth in the infancy narratives of Luke 1 and 2. (And let's not forget the prophetess Anna in Luke 2:36-38). More than any other Gospel, Luke tells us of Jesus' dealings with women (see Luke 7:11-17, 10:38-42, 13:10-17, 23:27-31) and only he tells us of the group of women who were associated with Jesus and the Twelve and who helped look after them (Luke 8:2, 3). All this implies an estimation of the value of women far higher than that which usually prevailed in the ancient world.

Luke shows no sign of being aware of any tension between what are frequently termed "evangelism" and "social action." If he is one of the writers of the New Testament who most strongly stresses social justice and social action, he is at the same time the one who is most interested in the missionary outreach of the Church! For Luke it is just as natural for believers to share their faith with others as it is for them to put it into practice, and just as natural for them to put their faith into practice as it is for them to share it with others.

The two volumes which make up Luke-Acts together account for over twenty-five percent of the New Testament. This in itself is an indication of their great importance. Although we know so little of "Luke" himself, we have him to thank not only for the most informative and attractive "Life of Jesus" ever written, but also for his profound insight into the way in which the life and work of Jesus are continued in the life and work of the Christian Church.

14. Acts of Apostles

The most remarkable thing about the Book of Acts is the very fact that it was written. The earliest generation of Christians had little or no need for written records. It was only as the original apostles began to die off that Mark took the step of writing an account of the Good News in what came to be known as a "Gospel." Sometime later, as we have seen, Luke also wrote an account of the life and ministry of Jesus but for him this was only the first volume of "The Origins of Christianity." Unlike the other Gospel writers Luke went on to compile a second volume which we know as the Book of Acts. He was one of the first to realize that the end of the world may be long delayed and that, in the present era of world history, the Christian Church has a key role to play in the unfolding purposes of God. Luke saw that not only the Christians of his day but also the Christians of the future would need to know how the Church began and what its true task is.

The introduction to Acts (1:1, 2) directs us back to the preface to the two-volume work in Luke 1:1-4. The reference in his Gospel to the use of earlier sources certainly applies to Acts as well. A probable explanation is that Luke, in the first part of Acts, made use of traditions or records preserved in important churches such as those at Jerusalem and Antioch. For the second part of Acts which deals mainly with Paul's travels, Luke certainly had other sources, including what appear to be extracts from the diary of one of Paul's companions. Read the passage which begins at Acts 16:6 and note how the story is told in the third person: "*they* went... when *they* had come... *they* attempted to go...." Now read on and notice the change that appears in verse 10: "Immediately *we* sought to go...." Events are now narrated in the first person ("we" instead of "they"), indicating that the writer was among those present at the time. This is true as far as verse 17 after which the use of "they" resumes. The diary reappears again in Acts 20:5-15, 21:1-18 and in 27:1 to 28:16. These are known as the "We" passages. Most scholars believe that these are extracts from Luke's own diary and that Luke himself was a travelling companion of Paul, at least towards the end of his career. Others think of the diary as one of the sources used by Luke; either way, it provides us with a particularly accurate and vivid series of pictures of the adventures of Paul.

A more controversial question concerns the speeches and sermons found in Acts. They occupy about thirty percent of the whole book. It was the accepted practice for Greek and Roman historians to compose speeches themselves and to write the kind of thing the character concerned might have said; some historians even used the speeches for putting across their own ideas. Some scholars maintain that the speeches in Acts are not verbatim accounts of what Peter or Paul actually said but, rather, Luke's own interpretation of the early Christian message. In support of this they argue that the speeches attributed to Paul contain very few of the expressions or ideas which are so characteristic of Paul's letters. Against this, however, can be placed evidence that Luke used sources here also, especially in the first part of Acts where the speeches show signs of translation from Aramaic and of a very early type of Christian theology. We do have to remember, however, that there were no cassette tape-recorders in New Testament times to record exactly what was said; moreover, the written speeches of Acts are really very short and can be regarded, at best, as summaries of what was said at the time.

Scholars who have been very sceptical about the historical accuracy of Acts as a whole have tended to ignore an impressive amount of evidence which points in the other direction. To give only one telling example, in recounting Paul's visit to Thessalonica in Acts 17:6, 8 Luke refers to "the city authorities" or local magistrates as *politarchai*. This Greek word is not used by Luke with reference to any other city; it was unknown in the whole of Greek literature before the modern discovery of several inscriptions from Thessalonica containing this very term. In other words, Luke (or his source) knew exactly the form of city government in Thessalonica at the time of Paul's visit.[20]

One thing we have to realize in reading the Book of Acts is the degree to which Luke was forced to *select* his material. We may wish that he had written twenty volumes but the fact is that he seems to have decided to write one standard-sized book (the same size as his Gospel). This means that a great deal had to be left out. Luke included what he thought was important, what he considered typical of the early Church, and what best served his aim in writing. The title of the book in Greek is "Acts of Apostles" (not "the" Acts of "the" Apostles) and this reminds us that, of the original twelve apostles, we really only hear about the acts of Peter (John has a walk-on part); even at that, Peter fades from the scene at Acts 12:17 with the tantalizing remark, "Then he departed and went to another place." We get some information on Stephen and Philip, while the second part of the book deals entirely with Paul's journeys. Even here there are large gaps: between Paul's departure to Tarsus (Acts 9:30) and his reappearance in Antioch (Acts 11:25, 26) there was probably a gap of nearly fourteen years (cf. Galatians 2:1); and if we read Acts 11:26, 18:11, 24:27 and 28:30 we discover that these four verses between them cover a combined total of six and a half years!

In Ever Widening Circles

What does Luke select and what does he emphasize as being of the first importance? Acts 1:8 provides us with an important clue, indeed almost with a table of contents for Acts. The risen Christ promises the apostles, "You shall receive power when the Holy Spirit has come upon you; and you shall be my witnesses in Jerusalem, and in all Judaea and Samaria, and to the end of the earth." After the introductory chapter, Acts can be divided into three main sections:

1) Witness in Jerusalem (chapters 2-7), with Peter and Stephen as the leading figures
2) Witness in Judaea and Samaria (8:1 — 11:18), with Philip and Peter as the leading figures

3) Witness to the Ends of the Earth (11:19 — 28:30), with Paul leading the mission to the Gentiles.

Selective though he has to be, Luke gives us a clear picture of the *spread* of early Christianity. At the first (Jerusalem) stage it is confined entirely to Jews but, at the second stage, in chapter 8, we witness an important development when the Gospel is preached to Samaritans whom most Jews considered to be half-breeds and heretics. Then, at the third stage, the big breakthrough comes when the message is taken to Gentiles and Christianity becomes a truly universal faith. Luke emphasizes the role of *Paul* as the one who was sent to the Gentiles "to open their eyes, that they may turn from darkness to light" (Acts 26:18). He thinks it tremendously important that *Peter* approved of the Gentile mission (albeit after much hesitation), as the key story of the conversion of the Roman centurion Cornelius demonstrates (10:1-11:18). But interestingly enough he preserves the information that the first approach to Gentiles was made at Antioch by some of the "Hellenist" Christians who were forced to flee from Jerusalem by the persecution which followed the death of Stephen (11:19-21; cf. 6:1-7, 8:1).

If Christianity spreads from Jews to Samaritans to Gentiles, it also spreads geographically, beginning in Jerusalem and moving outwards in ever-widening circles. Just as Luke's gospel both opens and closes in the great city of Jerusalem, so Acts begins in Jerusalem. It concludes, however, in the great city of Rome, the very capital of the Empire. Just as the last part of Luke's Gospel consists of a long journey by Jesus who had "set his face to go to *Jerusalem*" (Luke 9:51), so the last part of Acts consists of a long journey by Paul who has resolved, "I must also see *Rome*" (Acts 19:21). The universal nature of Christianity is further demonstrated by the way it is presented to all classes and conditions of people: to intellectuals at the University of Athens (17:16-34) and to a Roman governor (24:10-27), but also to a jailer (16:27-34) and to a demented slave girl (16:16-18). Here is a vision of the truly catholic or universal nature of the Church which must challenge the way Christians today so readily limit Christianity to their own national, ethnic or social group.

A Continuing Proclamation

This spread of the Good News is not presented as something carefully organized by a committee or planned in advance by ecclesiastical administrators, but as something inspired and directed by God himself. It has been well said that instead of "The Acts of the Apostles" a more appropriate title for the volume would be "The Acts of the Holy Spirit." Acts tells us of the giving of the Spirit to the Church on the day of Pentecost (Acts 2); whereas in Old Testament times the Spirit was given only occasionally and temporarily to certain individuals, the promised time has now come when all God's people receive the gift of the Spirit regardless of age, sex, social standing or any other distinction (Acts 2:17-21; cf. Joel 2:28-32). As in his Gospel, so also in Acts, Luke lays special emphasis on the role of women. Read through Acts carefully and note how often the Spirit fills Christians, speaks to them, guides them, instructs them, sends them, and even re-routes them when they are about to take off in the wrong direction (16:6)!

It has been suggested that Luke idealizes the early Church and that he divides its history into the "Age of the Apostles" when "the company of those who believed were of one heart and soul" (4:32), that is, when everything in the garden was lovely, and an "Age After the Apostles," in which he himself lived, when the Church was plagued by problems and divided by heresies as Paul foretells in 20:29, 30 ("Fierce wolves will come in among you, not sparing the flock; and from among your own selves will arise men speaking perverse things, to draw away the disciples after them").

There is certainly some truth in this view and, in his selection of material, Luke does omit or play down theological differences which did exist in the early Church. Paul's letters help give us a fuller and more realistic picture of the sometimes bitter controversies which raged even in his day. Yet, in emphasizing the unity and the fellowship, the dedication and the generosity, the joy and the enthusiasm of the first Christians, Luke is not portraying an impossible ideal but one which can and must be aimed at by his readers (in the twentieth century, as well as in the first).

The life of the early Church and even the life of Jesus provide an example which later ages can follow. While in one sense

Jesus' death on the cross was a unique and unrepeatable event, the account of Stephen's trial and death in Acts 6:11-15, 7:54-60 shows how Christians may be called upon to follow in the footsteps of their master. As Jesus died saying, "Father, forgive them; for they know not what they do" (found in Luke 23:34 but not in any of the other Gospels), so Stephen, the first Christian martyr, prays for his executioners, "Lord, do not hold this sin against them" (Acts 7:60). Stephen in his turn is held up as an example, reminding us that believers may at any time be called upon to sacrifice and suffer for their faith. Luke sees God at work throughout "salvation history," but the work of salvation is not just something prepared for in Old Testament times and accomplished in the life and ministry of Christ; it is something which continues to happen in the life of the Church and which, indeed, is still happening today.

One question has often puzzled the readers of Acts: why does the book end where it does? Paul has appealed to Caesar and has been taken to Rome to stand trial. "He lived there two whole years," we are told, during which time he was allowed to preach and teach. What we want to know, however, is what happened to Paul! For an answer we have to turn to later tradition according to which Paul was put to death, by beheading, on the Ostian Way just outside Rome in the persecution under Nero. (Another tradition holds that Paul was acquitted, undertook further travels, returned to Rome and only then suffered martyrdom). Why does Luke not narrate Paul's death? It has been suggested that Luke wrote Acts while Paul was still awaiting trial; he does not give the verdict because it has not yet been delivered. But this puts the writing of Acts impossibly early; there are strong reasons (for example, Luke's use of Mark) which rule out a date earlier than A.D. 70. It has also been suggested that Luke intended to write a *third* volume, but this is an even more unlikely suggestion. We can be sure that Luke knew of Paul's death (he drops some strong hints to this effect in Acts 20:24, 25 and 21:10-14) and that his readers knew also. But he *prefers* to end where he does with the Christian faith flourishing at the very centre of the Empire. Despite opposition and persecution, despite the fury of Nero which will be unleashed on the Church, the Kingdom of God is being preached. That is what counts and that is the right note on which to conclude. Here is the ground of hope, for our own day as well as for Luke's. Despite the crises and catastrophes which face our world, the proclamation of the Kingdom of God continues. If this undertaking were only human it would long since have failed (see Acts 5:38, 39); since it is of God, it cannot be overthrown.

The Writings of John

15. The Gospel According to John

For countless thousands of people the Gospel of John is the best loved book in the New Testament. Indeed, a case could probably be argued that this Gospel is one of the most influential books ever written in the whole of human history.

What is the secret of its wide appeal? It has been held that the Christian message is so simple that even a child can understand it, yet so profound that even the wisest person on earth could never exhaust its meaning. Such a verdict is particularly apt if applied to John's Gospel. Everyone can understand concepts such as life, light, bread, water, father, son, because these are universal symbols which relate not just to the first century A.D. Palestine but to the human situation. Not only is the Gospel written in terms which speak to people everywhere but its great themes are frequently repeated (with minor variations), so that if we do not get the message right away, it gradually sinks in as we read the Gospel chapter by chapter. There are many Christians who may not be able to follow the Nicene Creed but who would be quite happy to take as their summary of Christian faith, John 3:16 — "God so loved the world that he gave his only Son, that whoever believes in him should not perish but have eternal life."

This apparent simplicity is, of course, deceptive. The more saints and scholars have studied the Gospel, the more deep and profound they have discovered its meaning to be. One of the features of John's Gospel is that different levels of meaning can be found in the same passage or even the same expression. For example, in Jesus' dialogue with Nicodemus the phrase "born again" can also mean "born from above" (John 3:3); the Greek word for "wind" also means "spirit" (John 3:5-8); the allusion to the Son of Man being "lifted up" refers to Jesus' vindication and glorification by the Father and also to his being raised up on the cross (John 3:14). No wonder that numerous learned volumes have been written on "Johannine theology"!

Interpretation and Historicity in John

From an early date it has been recognized that John is concerned not just to state or re-state the facts of Jesus' ministry but to bring out their underlying meaning and significance. One of the early Church Fathers, Clement of Alexandria, writing about the end of the second century A.D., commented on the difference between John and the other three Gospels by saying: "Last of all, John, perceiving that the external facts had been made plain in the gospel, being urged by his friends, and inspired by the Spirit, composed a spiritual gospel."[21] Ever since then John has frequently been referred to as "the spiritual Gospel."

This becomes obvious the moment we read the opening verses. Mark is content to open his story with Jesus, as an adult, being baptized by John; this for him is "the beginning of the Gospel" (Mark 1:1). Matthew goes further back, to Jesus' birth and, indeed, traces Jesus' genealogy to Abraham, the father of God's chosen people. Luke goes further back still, tracing Jesus to Adam, to the very beginning of the human race.

But John goes even further back! The opening words of the Gospel ("In the beginning") are also the opening words of the Book of Genesis. John begins his account before human history, before the creation of the world even, and identifies Christ with the Word (the Greek term is *Logos*) who was with God in the beginning and through whom God created all things. In the Old Testament it is through his Word that God creates the universe and through his Word that he reveals himself to his people, Israel. God's "Word" and his "Wisdom" which exist before creation are close related. In Greek philosophy the Word

(Logos) meant the unifying, rational principle which permeates all reality. More so than the other Gospels John portrays Jesus' divine nature; he "pre-existed" as the only Son of the Father. But as John 1:14 puts it, "The Word became flesh and dwelt among us, full of grace and truth." A major emphasis in John's Gospel is thus what is known as the "Incarnation," which means literally "becoming flesh"; the divine Word and Son of God, in the person of Jesus, became a real human being.

John's concern with the underlying meaning of the Christ event has caused problems for some. At a number of points John's Gospel does not agree with the other three. Perhaps the most striking example of this is found in the timing of the Last Supper. Mark, followed by Matthew and Luke, clearly presents the Supper as the Jewish Passover meal. But John dates the sequence of events exactly twenty-four hours earlier so that the Supper is held the night *before* Passover. Now the effect of this is that, in John's Gospel, Jesus is dying on the cross at the very time when the Passover lambs are being slain in the Temple. When we remember that it is in John that Jesus is described as "the Lamb of God, who takes away the sin of the world" (John 1:29, 36), it is difficult to avoid the conclusion that John was not fussy about exact chronology but that he was tremendously concerned to have his readers understand the meaning of Jesus' death as a sacrifice for the sins of the world.

This raises the question, however, of just how far John was concerned with history and with historical accuracy. The teaching of Jesus in John is markedly different from the other three Gospels where Jesus teaches by means of vivid parables and short, striking, pithy sayings. In John there are no parables at all, and Jesus gives long and quite elaborate discourses. Often, it is difficult to say where the words of Jesus leave off and the meditation of the writer begins. John 3:16 is a case in point: are these words of Jesus (remember, there were no inverted commas in ancient manuscripts to show where direct speech begins and ends) or are they the writer's interpretation of the Christ event just as, for example, Paul can say, "God was in Christ reconciling the world to himself" (II Cor 5:19)?

No one can dispute the strong element of interpretation in John, and it is exactly this that raises the question of his attitude to history. Over the past hundred years some scholars have gone so far as to argue that John is not really interested in history at all, that there is very little history in his Gospel.

In view of this certain points must be noted. One is that much recent research has tended to support the basic historicity of the Gospel. Archaeological discoveries, for example, have suggested that the Gospel shows a remarkably accurate knowledge of the geography of Palestine. It has generally been held that John has some knowledge of the other Gospels (certainly Mark, probably Luke, possibly Matthew) and borrows from them. More recently the view has been gaining ground that John's Gospel is quite independent of the others, but that it has access to its own sources, such as a "Signs Source" (recounting miracles of Jesus) and an early version of the passion narrative. While the Gospel was once generally regarded as typically "Greek," and therefore remote from the Jesus of history, recent studies have shown how much it depends on the Old Testament and reflects the Jewish thought of the period.

Few today would dismiss the Gospel as historically worthless. At the same time most contemporary scholars recognize *both* the use of historical traditions *and* the strong element of interpretation. It is surely no coincidence the "spiritual Gospel" contains the five key passages promising the disciples that, after Jesus' departure, they would receive the gift of the Spirit (or Paraclete) who would guide them into all truth (see John 14:16, 17, 14:26, 15:26, 16:7-11, 16:13-15). John does not simply repeat facts; under the promised guidance of the Spirit he unfolds the deeper meaning of Jesus' life and death for the Church of his day — and of today.

The Authorship Debate

It comes as a surprise to some people to discover that this Gospel, like the other three, is anonymous: nowhere in the text is the author named. Equally surprising is the uncertainty which surrounded the Gospel in the early Church: as late as A.D. 200 questions were being raised about its authorship and even about whether it should be accepted by the Church. The earliest traditions name the writer simply as "John" (a common name then as now), designate him as a "disciple" of Jesus and link him with the city of Ephesus. In the late second century A.D. writers begin to identify "John" with John the apostle, the brother of

James and the son of Zebedee. This became the traditional view and it is still widely held and strongly defended by many to the present day. Honesty compels us to admit, however, that this view presents certain difficulties.

The question of authorship is bound up with the identity of the mysterious "disciple whom Jesus loved," mentioned in John 13:23-25, 19:26, 27, 20:2-10, 21:7 and 21:20-24. John 21:24 seems to identify this "beloved disciple" with the writer of the Gospel, yet in none of these passages is he named or identified! The "beloved disciple" is depicted as being very close to Jesus, although he appears on the scene only at the very end of Jesus' life. Traditionally, he has been identified as John, the son of Zebedee, since in the first three Gospels this John appears as one of the twelve disciples. This would seem to qualify him as one of the few men who would have the kind of "inside knowledge" we find in John's Gospel.

This theory, however, has a major snag. The apostle John is indeed one of a small group present at the healing of Peter's mother-in-law (Mark 1:29), the raising of Jairus' daughter (Mark 5:37), the Transfiguration (Mark 9:2), the discourse on the signs of the end (Mark 13:3), the preparations for the Passover (Luke 22:8), and the agony in Gethsemane (Mark 14:33). Yet none of these events is even mentioned in John's Gospel, an omission which seems incredible if the apostle John was indeed "the beloved disciple"!

We cannot, therefore, be certain who this "beloved disciple" was: the Gospel itself does not tell us and there are problems with the traditional identification. One other suggestion is that he was Lazarus since he is referred to as one whom Jesus loved in John 11:3.

It is not even one hundred percent certain that the "beloved disciple" actually wrote the Gospel himself. John 21:24 may suggest, rather, that he was an eye-witness of the life of Jesus and the *source* of the author's information. In this case the actual author would be a later writer or editor, perhaps "John the Presbyter" (or Elder) who lived in Ephesus near the end of the first century and who seems to be distinguished from John the apostle by the early Christian writer Papias.[22]

Many Christians prefer to stick with the traditional view that the apostle John wrote the Gospel despite the difficulties this involves; others are content to admit that we cannot know for sure who the author was and recognize that we do not need to be too concerned over the matter.

It is interesting to note some recent trends which are even supported by scholars who do not believe that John the apostle wrote the Gospel. One such trend is towards a much earlier dating; recently a date before A.D. 70 has been defended by several scholars. Others would place the writing of the Gospel in Syria or even Palestine rather than in the more faraway Ephesus.

Recently a number of scholars have suggested that John's Gospel may not have been written entirely by one person at one time; rather, it may be the end product of a lengthy and possibly complicated process of development. The Johannine traditions may have originated with the Jerusalem-based "Hellenists" (Acts 6) who were forced to flee following the death of Stephen and who undertook a mission to the Samaritans in whom the Gospel shows a special interest. The distinctive Johannine theology may have developed among these dispersed groups which came into conflict with continuing followers of John the Baptist as well as with Jewish synagogue authorities. The Gospel appears to have been published in a first edition consisting of chapters 1-20; chapter 21 is an appendix added to a second edition of the Gospel.

These theories thus posit the existence an ongoing "Johannine community" or "Johannine school," which represents one of a number of branches of the early Church. Consensus on these matters has not yet been reached and discussions continue to be lively!

The Judgment Is Now

One of the most striking features of John's Gospel is its constant use of pairs of opposites: light and darkness, life and death, truth and error. Those who held that this kind of thought did not exist in Palestine were surprised to find very similar language used in the Dead Sea Scrolls which were written in Palestine prior to Jesus' day. (In other ways, however, the Scrolls are very different from the New Testament.) John sees history as a drama in which conflicting powers battle with each other: the light shines in the darkness (John 1:5), the believer passes from death to life (John 5:24), the devil has nothing to do with the truth for he is the father of lies (John 8:44). As in John's time, so in our own, the forces of darkness, death and error so often look as if they are going to carry the day. John, however, assures his readers that with the coming of Jesus the decisive battle has already been fought and won. He *is* the Light of the world (John 8:12), the Truth and the Life (John 14:6). "The light shines in the darkness, and the darkness has not overcome it" (John 1:5). "Be of good cheer," says Jesus, "I have overcome the world" (John 16:33).

Light and darkness, life and death, truth and error do not simply represent a great cosmic struggle taking place "out there"; they are possibilities for each individual. It is possible for people to "walk" in the light or in the darkness (John 12:35, 36), to have life or not have life (John 5:24), to "do the truth" or not do the truth (John 3:21). What is required on the part of those who hear the message is to believe. John never uses the abstract noun "faith," but again and again uses the verb "believe." "He who believes in the Son has eternal life" (John 3:36). The purpose for which the Gospel is written is said to be "that you may believe that Jesus is the Christ, the Son of God, and that believing you may have life in his name" (John 20:31).

In Jewish expectation, events such as the Judgment, the Resurrection and eternal life lay in the future and were connected with the end of history and with the coming of the Messiah. In John these are present realities, for the Messiah has indeed come! "Now is the judgment" (John 12:31) and people are judged here and now if they love darkness rather than light (John 3:19). Jesus is the Resurrection and the Life (John 11:25) and the believer has already passed from death to life (John 5:24). "He who believes in the Son has eternal life" (John 3:36). Nothing could indicate more clearly that "eternal" life does not refer simply to unending duration. It is a matter of the *quality* of life, not the *quantity*. Jesus offers believers true life, real life, the life which is life indeed, and they can begin to experience it here and now! John does not entirely eliminate a future expectation (see John 5:25-29) but, for him, it is the encounter with Christ in the present which is decisive.

From the way in which John' Gospel sometimes refers to "this world" it might be concluded that what is being advocated is a very "other-worldly" form of religion which turns its back on the world's problems and needs. The devil is called "the ruler of this world" (John 14:30), and the disciples are told that the world will hate them just as it hates Jesus (John 15:18, 19). The Christian Church has often been tempted to retreat from the world (something which can happen in a Protestant prayer group as well as in a Roman Catholic monastery). We do well, therefore, to remember that John also asserts that God created the world, loved it and sent his Son to save it. The "world," in the bad sense, means humankind insofar as it rebels against God and disobeys his will. While believers are not to accept this world's standards and values, neither are they to insulate themselves against this world's problems and needs. "I do not pray that thou shouldst take them out of the world", prays Jesus, "but that thou shouldst keep them from evil... As thou didst send me into the world, so I have sent them into the world" (John 17:15, 18).

This is a tough task but it is one, John tells us, for which Jesus sought to prepare his disciples. The term "Church" does not appear in John's Gospel, but the reality is there in the little community which Jesus gathered and taught (see especially chapters 13 to 17), the group consisting of his "disciples," his "friends," his "own." Through this group Christ speaks to Christians today, giving them an example of humble and unselfish service (John 13:15) and assuring them that, just as the branch cannot bear fruit unless it abides in the vine, so it is only by abiding in Christ that they can find the strength they need for Christian living and can know the love and joy which are to be the keynotes of the Christian life (John 15:1-17).

16. The Letters of John

In a day which has seen the rise of all kinds of new sects and cults, in which it is difficult to keep pace with the latest "new theology" or "new morality," in which Christian theologians can write of *The Myth of God Incarnate,* it is small wonder that many Christians are perplexed and ask such questions as: "How does a Christian know what to believe?" or "How does a Christian know how to live?" or even, "How do I know whether I truly am a Christian?" Within the churches there are people who claim to "know Christ" or to have received the gift of the Spirit but whose lives do not seem to support such claims. Even Jim Jones, the founder of the "People's Temple," claimed to be a teacher of God's truth, yet he did not lead his followers in the way of life but to a horrible death in the jungles of Guyana.

The Problem of False Teaching

How do we know who is speaking the truth? This is not a new problem because this question bothered the Christians for whom the letters of John were written. It is sometimes said that I John is not really a letter because it has neither opening nor closing greetings and no personal names or details. Perhaps it was written for a group of churches so that a messenger could read it to each one. The writer is clearly a Church leader in a position of authority. Equally clearly, he is dealing with a specific crisis in the life of the congregations concerned. A false teaching has arisen and many Christians have become attracted to it. So serious is the distortion of Christian truth involved that the writer labels the group "antichrists" (I John 2:18). The notion that, before the end of the world, evil will have a final fling led by a person or creature who represents all that is anti (against)-God and anti-Christ occurs several places in the Bible. Those who follow the false teaching represent this power which works against God's purposes. Evidently, matters had come to a head and they had split with the congregation and presumably formed a new group on their own: "They went out from us, but they were not of us" (I John 2:19). We may see nothing startling about this because we can look back on the sad story of nearly 2000 years of Church history during which,

> "Men see her sore opprest,
> By schisms rent asunder,
> By heresies distrest."

But we must remember that this was probably the first split in the Christian Church. Those who remained behind were still suffering from the shock and, moreover, they were anxious to know whether they had done the right thing. The false teachers no doubt sounded very plausible: how was the ordinary Christian to know truth from error? I John was written to support these Christians in the stand they had taken for the truth and to help them cope with a difficult situation.

II and III John are short notes (each one would exactly fill one sheet of papyrus). II John begins, "The Elder to the elect lady and her children...." Most scholars agree that "the elect lady" means a Christian church while the "children" are the members of the congregation; the "elect sister" in verse 13 would refer to the writer's own church, thought of as a "sister congregation" of the recipients. The letter mentions briefly the same false teachers who appear in I John; anyone who follows this teaching is a "deceiver" and "antichrist" (verse 7). The difference here is that the false teaching does not appear to have yet struck this congregation. Perhaps they were a distance away, up-country and so could be warned ahead of time not to receive anyone who comes to them and does not "abide in the doctrine of Christ" (verse 9).

III John is different again because it is written to an individual called Gaius, a loyal member of another congregation, where there had occurred something all too frequent in the later history of the Church — a "row" in which personalities were involved. It appears that the writer of the letters had sent out a group of "brothers" on a kind of preaching tour, probably under the leadership of the Demetrius who is mentioned in verse 12. In this particular congregation there was another man named Diotrephes who was against receiving the travelling preachers and who convinced others of his point of view. Obviously, church politics were involved here: Diotrephes appears as a kind of "congregationalist" who thinks each congregation should run its own affairs and declares that "no outsider is going to come in and dictate to us!" No doubt he had his own personal ambitions; we are told that he "likes to put himself first" (verse 9). It is not clear how far the dispute was theological as well as personal, but the way the writer keeps emphasizing "the truth," an expression which is frequent in I and II John, suggests that Diotrephes may have had some connection with the false teachers.

III John, then, is written from the point of view that a local congregation is only part of the wider body of Christ and that, where problems arise, some kind of guidance and oversight from the Church as a whole needs to be given to local groups to ensure that they do not stray from "the truth."

It is obvious that the three letters of John stand in a very close relationship to John's Gospel because they share so many ideas and expressions. As with the Gospel, so also with the Letters, there appears to have been doubt regarding their authorship and authority in the earliest days of the Church. In time, however, it came to be held that all four works had been written by the apostle John. This became the traditional view. Actually, the three letters (like the Gospel) are anonymous: the writer nowhere identifies himself by name. In both II John and III John he does introduce himself as "the Elder." This would be strange if he was in fact an apostle since we would expect him to claim the more important title, especially as in this difficult situation he wishes to assert his authority. As we have seen, evidence suggests that in Ephesus, towards the end of the first century, there lived a "John the Elder" (or Presbyter), a person quite distinct from John the Apostle. Some scholars, therefore, regard this John the Elder as the author of the letters.

Not all scholars, however, agree that the letters were written by the same person who wrote John's Gospel. Despite the close similarities there are also some differences both in style and thought, as C. H. Dodd[23] and others have pointed out. The letters lay more stress on Christ's death as an atonement for sin, on his second coming and on a future judgment. These differences could be explained if the letters were written some time after the Gospel (almost certainly it was this way round) and if, as a number of recent scholars have argued, the letters were written to correct certain misunderstandings of the false teachers. In order to correct this situation, it was necessary to shift the emphasis at certain points. Another much discussed suggestion is that the Gospel and letters may come, if not from the same author, at least from the same "Johannine school" or "Johannine community" within early Christianity, perhaps a group of congregations sharing common traditions and a common interpretation of the Christian faith.

What exactly was the false teaching that was causing all the trouble in the churches to which the letters were written? Most scholars see it as an early form of Gnosticism. Its adherents regarded the material universe and the human body as essentially evil. They could accept that Christ was a spiritual being, an angelic messenger sent from God, but they did not believe that he had truly become a human being. One such early Gnostic called Cerinthus had the extraordinary idea that the spiritual Christ came down upon the earthly Jesus in the form of the dove at the baptism but then left Jesus and went back to heaven before his suffering and death![24] This view is also known as "Docetism" (from the Greek word meaning "to seem"); it alleged that Christ only *seemed* to be a man. These people just could not accept that the Son of God took on human flesh and truly entered our world of sin and suffering.

The Gnostics thought of themselves as a class apart from and above ordinary Christians, and this seems to be true of the group referred to in I John. They laid claim to an intellectual superiority and may also have claimed to have received a special anointing of the Spirit (cf. I John 2:20, 27) — not the only example of "spiritual snobbery" to be found in the history of the Christian church!

Finally, members of this group seem to have made the claim, "We have no sin" (I John 1:8, 10), by which they probably meant that the ordinary rules did not apply to them. They had deceived themselves into thinking that, since they belonged to the spiritual elite, they did not have to be concerned with standards like the Ten Commandments which were only for Christians at a lower level.

Suggestions for Discerning the Truth

No wonder ordinary believers were perplexed. You could not believe everybody who claimed to possess God's Spirit. It is necessary, the writer tells them, to "test the spirits to see whether they are of God" (I John 4:1), and he suggests to them a series of tests which can be applied, introducing each of these with some such formula as, "By this we know..." or "By this we may be sure..." One of the older but still valuable books on the letters of John, written by Robert Law and published in 1909, is entitled *The Tests of Life.*[25] The tests which are outlined in I John are still of fundamental importance and can be applied by Christians today. They are of two kinds: tests of right belief and tests of right conduct.

At the heart of *right belief* is the acknowledgement that Jesus is the Christ or promised Messiah (I John 5:1) and the Son of God (I John 4:15). In the situation which lies behind the letters, however, the acid test was confessing that "Jesus Christ has come in the flesh" (I John 4:2; II John 7). In Christ, God truly entered into human history. We can be assured of redemption only if Christ truly became one of us and truly suffered and died "for the sins of the whole world" (I John 2:2). He came not just "with the water," that is, by submitting to baptism but also "with the blood," that is, by submitting to the cross (I John 5:6).

Right belief has to be matched by *right conduct.* "By this we may be sure that we know him, if we keep his commandments..." (I John 2:3), if we "walk in the same way in which he [Jesus] walked" (I John 2:6) and if we do what is right (I John 2:29). Here is the practical test which must be applied, and the writer of I John certainly does not mince his words: "He who says 'I know him' but disobeys his commandments is a liar, and the truth is not in him" (I John 2:4).

The Love of God

Of course the writer is not talking of cold, intellectual belief or of legalistic observance of the commandments because, for him, *love* is the key to Christian thought and life. The starting point of love is with God: "We love, because he first loved us" (I John 4:19). If we ask where we see God's love most clearly shown, then the answer is in the sending of Jesus to be the Saviour of the world (I John 4:14). Christ is the supreme expression of totally unselfish, self-sacrificing love. "By this we know love, that he laid down his life for us" (I John 3:16). Must not such a love evoke a response? "Beloved, if God so loved us, we also ought to love one another" (I John 4:11). The commandment that must govern the lives of Christians goes right back to Christ himself — "that we love one another" (II John 5). Once again the writer goes straight to the point and speaks directly to a world divided between the "have" nations and the "have-nots": "If any one has the world's goods and sees his brother in need, yet closes his heart against him, how does God's love abide in him?" (I John 3:17).

The style of I John is a bit repetitious. There is no agreement on the outline of the letter, and you will find a different one in each commentary you consult. A number of recent scholars have tried to detect an earlier source or document lying behind the letter but their efforts have not won much acceptance. It is possible that I John is based on a sermon. Sermons can be somewhat rambling (perhaps you've noticed) and this one certainly was not a snappy "three-pointer." Perhaps the writer used some earlier sermon notes and worked them up into a letter.

There is one passage in I John which has caused problems. In 5:16, 17 the writer distinguishes between mortal sins (literally sins "unto death") and sins which are not mortal (not "unto death," also known as "venial" sins). He encourages the readers to pray for a fellow Christian committing what is not a mortal sin but adds, "There is a sin which is mortal; I do not say that one is to pray for that." Unfortunately he does not tell us what kind of sin belongs to each category. In speaking of mortal sins it is unlikely that he had in mind specific sins such as murder or adultery as has sometimes been suggested. Jewish thought sometimes distinguished between unwitting sin and sin committed "with a high hand" (cf. Numbers 15:29, 30). This may be partly what is in mind here. Most probably people commit the sin "unto death" when quite knowingly and deliberately they renounce their faith in Christ. Someone who consciously refuses to believe in Christ or obey God's commands, or whose life is completely lacking in love, is cut off from the sphere of life. The one person who cannot receive God's forgiveness is the person who arrogantly and falsely claims to be sinless. There is a sense in which such a person is past praying for. Yet, surely, what is said here does not rule out the possibility that God's grace could still reach such people and restore them to life.

There is much of value to Christians today in these letters, especially the great summary of Christian belief expressed so simply yet so profoundly in I John 4:16: "God is love, and he who abides in love abides in God, and God abides in him."

17. The Letter to the Hebrews

The Letter to the Hebrews has never been the most popular book of the New Testament and, indeed, for most Christians, it is not even in the top ten. A quick glance at the letter, filled with Old Testament quotations and discussions of priesthood and sacrifice, suggests that it is obscure and irrelevant. Apart, perhaps, from reading the eleventh chapter at an anniversary service the book is generally neglected. This is a great pity and a great loss for the Church. Hebrews demands careful reading and study, but such effort will be amply repaid. If we are prepared to try, we shall certainly discover behind the unfamiliar language and ideas an original and independent interpretation of the Christian message which has much to say to the Church at the present time.

It may be that readers are put off by the uncertainty regarding both the author and the original recipients of the letter. After much hesitation (especially in the West), it was eventually ascribed to Paul, a tradition found for example in the *King James Version* which labelled it "The Epistle of Paul the Apostle to the Hebrews." However, the letter does not claim to be by Paul, and the language, style and ideas are so different from what we find in his letters that authorship by Paul is out of the question. This fact was recognized by some scholars in the early Church and at the time of the Reformation, as well as by a majority of modern scholars. A "Guess the Author" contest has been going on for a long time! It is a sign of the times that the modern (Roman Catholic) Jerusalem Bible is inclined to favour Apollos (see Acts 18:24-28), the candidate first suggested by Martin Luther. A more recent suggestion is that it might have been written by a woman, Priscilla. In the end we still have to come back to the verdict of Origen, the great third century biblical scholar: "As to who wrote the letter, the truth is — God only knows."[26]

The destination of the letter is also uncertain. The phrase, "Those who come from Italy send you greetings" (13:24), could mean that the letter was written either *to* or *from* an Italian church (most likely Rome). Nonetheless, a careful reading of the letter reveals quite a lot about the group of Christians to whom it was written. They were not eye-witnesses to the life of Jesus but were converted by those who were (2:3). Some considerable period of time has elapsed since their conversion. Their former leaders are apparently dead (13:7) and by this time they should have made considerable progress in the Christian faith (though in fact they have not — 5:12-14). They have had to suffer harassment and imprisonment but not martyrdom (12:4). There are some indications that the readers formed a small group within a larger community (cf. 13:24) and may well have constituted a "house church" within a larger city congregation. They have clearly lost their original enthusiasm and settled down into a comfortable complacency. They are in danger in "falling away from the living God" (3:12) and of drifting away from the message of the Gospel (2:1). The writer complains even about the falling off in attendance at worship (10:25)! It is not too difficult to identify parallels between the situation of the readers of the letter and the situation which confronts many Christian congregations today.

A Call for Deeper Personal Commitment

The writer seeks to bring about the *renewal* of the Church. This letter contains both theological instruction and practical application (in Greek *paraklēsis*, usually translated as "exhortation"). Blocks of exhortation keep breaking into the theological argument as if the writer were saying, "This is not an exercise in academic theology; this has a vital bearing on the whole life and work of the Church." In 13:22 the writer calls his letter "a word of exhortation" and most recent commentators recognize that the exhortations are the main point of the epistle. The author's chief purpose is to lift up the drooping hands and to strengthen the weak knees (12:12).

How is this renewal in the life of the Church to come about? Not by appointing a new committee or by re-structuring the Boards of the Church! The writer has remarkably little interest in Church organization. Evidently, he does not think that renewal can be imposed from above; rather, it will come about only through a deeper theological understanding and a deeper personal commitment at the grassroots level. He is not one of those who says, "Never mind theology, let's get on with the work of the Church." Instead he sees that the only way to revitalize the Church is by rediscovering and reappropriating the essential message of the Good News of God's grace in Jesus Christ. The author's prescription is not *less* but *more* and *better* theology.

The diagnosis of what is basically wrong in the Church is found in 5:12: "Though by this time you ought to be teachers, you need someone to teach you the ABC of God's oracles over again; it has come to this, that you need milk instead of solid food" (*New English Bible*). In other words, his readers are theologically illiterate; what they desperately need is adult Christian education. So what else is new? If Christians today persist in regarding Christian education as kids' stuff, something to be abandoned at age ten (if not earlier), how can they be surprised that so many Church members fail to manifest a mature, informed adult faith?

In the opening chapter the writer seems to be countering various erroneous or at least inadequate conceptions of Christ which were going the rounds. It is inaccurate to picture Christ as a kind of angel, simply one of a series of divine messengers (1:5-2:18). Jesus is not simply a great prophet and teacher like Moses (3:1-6), nor is he simply a nationalistic leader like Joshua under whom the Israelites settled in Palestine (4:1-10). There may be some truth in each of these ways of looking at Jesus but, if the readers stop there, they will have only a very imperfect and inadequate grasp of the person and work of Christ.

A New Relationship Established

Hebrews sees the life, death and resurrection of Jesus as the great turning-point of human history. Christ makes possible a new relationship between God and human beings. Back in the days of Moses God entered into a covenant or special relationship with the people of Israel; he would be their God and they would respond by living in accordance with his Law, especially the Ten Commandments, given at Mount Sinai.

That's not the way things worked out and, time and again, Israel rebelled against God. The great prophet, Jeremiah, saw that the only hope lay in a new covenant or new relationship in which the people's sin would be forgiven and in which they would truly love God in their hearts and obey God in their lives (Jeremiah 31:31-34, quoted in full in Hebrews 8:8-12). What Jeremiah longed for has now become a reality! Christ has made possible this new relationship with God by bringing into being the new covenant or, as the word can also be translated, the new "testament." The laws and the rituals of the old covenant or testament were only a preparation for the coming of the new covenant or testament; they were "but a shadow of the good things to come" (10:1). Here is where we get the basic distinction between the Old Testament and the New Testament as well as guidance on what the Christian attitude towards the Old Testament ought to be.

How has Jesus made possible this new relationship with God? Here the author really strikes out on his own in portraying Jesus as the great High Priest. Of course, technically, Jesus was not a priest at all since Jewish priests had to be descended from the tribe of Levi and Jesus was of the tribe of Judah (a fact which qualified him as the expected Messiah of David's line). Hebrews is well aware of this: "It is evident that our Lord was descended from Judah, and in connection with that tribe Moses said nothing about priests" (7:14). But he is not worried: the mysterious figure of the priest-king Melchizedek (mentioned in Genesis 14:18-20) provides a precedent for a great priest who was not from the tribe of Levi. Indeed, Melchizedek foreshadows Christ himself.

A priest is someone who bridges the gap between God and humanity (the Latin word for priest is *pontifex* which literally means "bridge-builder"). The Old Testament priests represented God to the people only in a very limited and imperfect way because they themselves were human and sinful. Christ, however, can truly represent God to us because he is the sinless Son of God; in Christ, God directly reaches out to people in grace and mercy.

A priest must also represent the people before God. This is where the idea of Jesus as "high priest" allows the writer to demonstrate how Christ is both fully divine and fully human. "He had to be made like his brothers in every respect, so that he might become a merciful and faithful high priest" (2:17). Jesus shared the full range of human experience with only this one difference: while he faced all the temptations we have to face, he never *yielded* to temptation. "We have not a high priest who is unable to sympathize with our weaknesses, but one who in every respect has been tempted as we are, yet without sinning" (4:15). To "sympathize" means literally "to suffer along with" someone and that is exactly what Christ has done. In our doubts and fears, crises and anguish, Christ knows and understands because he's been through it himself. Indeed, he suffers along with humanity.

Broken relationships can be restored only through costly self-giving. Christ's death on the cross, as well as his whole life of obedience to God, is seen as a sacrifice which renders obsolete the whole Jewish system of animal sacrifice and which inaugurates the new covenant, opening up for all "the new and living way" to God (10:20). Christ is now exalted to heaven where he continually prays for all people and makes it possible for them to draw near to God.

God's Pilgrim People

What should be the response to this? Christians can never earn or deserve "such a great salvation" (2:3), but they are called to respond in faith and, through faith, to be strengthened for service. For Hebrews this faith is never a purely individual thing. Believers take their place in a whole succession of men and women of faith reviewed in chapter eleven.

The tremendous picture of the Church in this letter has been well summed up in the title of an important study by the German scholar, Ernst Käsemann, called *The Wandering People of God.*[27] The true people of God live by faith, are willing to abandon earthly security, are prepared to defy convention, break with the establishment and march boldly into the unknown future, like Abraham who "went out, not knowing where he was to go" (11:8). What, one wonders, would the writer have to say about the conservative, traditionalist and "in group" mentality of so many present-day Christian congregations?

Read through chapter eleven and you will discover that the writer picks heroes and heroines rather carefully, concentrating on the patriarchs and Moses, barely mentioning David and omitting Solomon, the builder of the Temple. The author's heroes and heroines lived in tents (11:9), and he definitely loses interest when they started pouring concrete! What does this have to say to a downtown church spending a disproportionate amount of its income on the upkeep of an ancient, Gothic structure or to a new suburban congregation contemplating taking on a large mortgage?

Faith is thus the all-essential element in the Christian life, but growth and development are important also. In the *King James Version* of 6:1 the author exhorts us to "go on unto perfection." Most people do not find that very helpful advice; we tend to say "nobody's perfect," and so dismiss this as an impossible ideal. However, the Greek word here *(teleiotēs)* is helpfully rendered by most modern translations as "maturity." Christians are not expected to achieve some kind of abstract perfection but they are challenged to develop towards maturity. Mature Christians are those who can make responsible moral decisions for themselves (see 5:14) because through both Christian education and Christian experience they have reached an adult level of Christian discipleship.

The writer of Hebrews does not discuss the issue of "faith" and "works" such as we find in Paul and in the Letter of James. He assumes that faith must manifest itself in love and in service to others and he frequently reminds his readers of this. Christians no longer offer sacrifices in the Temple at Jerusalem because their whole lives will be characterized by self-sacrificing love: "Do not neglect to do good and to share what you have, for such sacrifices are pleasing to God" (13:16). He exhorts his readers to "Let brotherly love continue" (13:1) and goes on to give examples of some of the keynotes of the Christian life-style: showing hospitality to strangers, visiting those in prison, honouring the marriage relationship, keeping free from love of money (13:2-5). At a couple of points the letter strikes a very stern note: those who deliberately persist in sin cannot avoid God's judgment (6:4-8, 10:26-31). The writer is probably thinking here of those who are tempted to give up their Christian faith altogether whenever the going gets rough. When believers publicly deny their Lord they are in effect crucifying him over again (6:6).

Our Life Reflects Our Faith

Faith and works, religion and ethics, cannot be separated; how we live depends on what we believe. This is clearly illustrated in a passage such as 10:19-25 which begins by summing up the main theological points which have been made: through the sacrifice of Christ, the great High Priest, believers can have free access to God. This is immediately followed up by three exhortations: "Let us draw near (to God) with a true heart in full assurance of faith" (10:22); "Let us hold fast the confession of our hope without wavering" (10:23); and, "Let us consider how to stir up one another to love and good works" (10:24). The Greek word the writer uses here *(paroxysmos)* is a strong one which can mean either to provoke or to stimulate. From it comes the English word "paroxysm" which the dictionary defines as "a sudden violent emotion or action." What the phrase literally says is, "Let us be concerned with one another to produce a paroxysm of love and good deeds!" If Christians really grasped what Christ has done for them, then they would be galvanized into action!

Hebrews is a difficult book to understand, but if we make the effort, we will be rewarded by a vision of Christ as the great High Priest, of the Church as God's pilgrim people and of the kind of Christian maturity to which believers are called.

18.
The Letter of James

No book of the New Testament has had such a mixed reception as the Letter of James. Up to about A.D. 200 no early Christian writer even quotes from James. It was not firmly accepted as belonging in the New Testament until well into the fourth century, although even after that there were those who had their doubts. Then, at the time of the Reformation in the sixteenth century, came the remarkable attack by Martin Luther. His famous verdict was that James is "a right strawy epistle" which has "nothing of the gospel about it."[28] Because the work "contains not a syllable about Christ" and does not even mention the Cross, the Resurrection or the Holy Spirit, Luther would have been quite happy to have it excluded from the New Testament. In modern times, many have been influenced by these earlier doubts. They point to the differences between James and Paul as a clear example not just of diversity within the New Testament but of outright contradiction.

On the other hand, there certainly are some people (perhaps more than care to admit it) who are rather fond of James because it is easy to understand and because it provides some quite straightforward and practical teaching on Christian living. Take the little picture that is painted in 2:1-7. A rich visitor enters the church with fine clothes and gold rings at the same time as a poor man in shabby clothing comes in off the street.

We can imagine the usher on duty bowing and scraping as he leads the rich man to the best seat available, all the time sizing up how much he is likely to put in the offering plate, while the poor man (when the usher eventually gets round to him) is told to stand at the back or to sit on the floor. What a powerful condemnation, albeit in capsule form, of the kind of snobbery and social distinctions which ought to have *no* place within a Christian congregation!

Or consider the snapshot in 4:13 of the meeting of business executives planning to expand their merchandising operations and calculating future profits, all as if God never existed. What a jolting reminder of the shortness and uncertainty of human life! None of us can control the future and all our plans must carry the all-important proviso of "God willing."

Or consider yet another passage with a very modern ring about it, 2:14-16. "If a brother or sister is ill-clad and in lack of daily food, and one of you says to them, 'Go in peace, be warmed and filled,' without giving them the things needed for the body, what does it profit?" What good are pious platitudes to refugees or the starving or the latest victims of hurricane or earthquake? There is a directness and practicality about the Letter of James which many Christians prefer to a work full of abstract theological arguments and incomprehensible language.

Apply Your Faith to Your Daily Lives

Whether we like it or not James is part of the New Testament and it deserves careful study. What kind of work is it? The opening greeting in 1:1 suggests that it is a letter: "James... to the twelve tribes in the Dispersion: Greeting." The rest of the book, however, has none of the characteristics of, let us say, the letters of Paul. There are no concluding greetings nor anything to suggest that it is addressed to a particular congregation at any one particular place or time. The situations dealt with in the letter are *typical* ones which could arise anywhere.

James is much more like a sermon than a letter. It is not the kind of sermon which challenges the listeners to decision and commitment; rather, it assumes that the listeners are already believers and exhorts them to live up to their faith and to apply it in their daily lives. Scholars refer to this by the Greek term *parainesis* which means a homily or, if you like, a pep-talk. The writer seems to ramble on from one topic to another, although frequently there is some connection between one section and the next. In a couple of cases, the same topic recurs later in the letter. See, for example, the selections on the dangers of the tongue in 1:26, 3:1-12 and 4:11, 12, and on the condemnation of the rich in 1:9-11, 2:1-7 and 5:1-6. In these passages the writer is using the same principle as radio and television commercials: drive home your point by repetition at frequent intervals.

This kind of practical sermon often circulated in written form. It is similar to the "Wisdom Literature" of the Old Testament such as the Book of Proverbs, or Sirach (Ecclesiasticus) in the Apocrypha. In the Greek world, too, lists of duties and ethical teachings were popular. In the New Testament itself we find collections of practical sayings, for example, in the Sermon on the Mount or at the end of some of Paul's letters. James, however, is the only book in the New Testament to consist of this kind of material and nothing else.

Can we say who the author was? He identifies himself simply as James, a common name then as now. He claims only to be "a servant of God and of the Lord Jesus Christ" (1:1) and a teacher (see 3:1). Eusebius, the famous Church historian writing in the early fourth century,[29] was the first to suggest that the author was James, the brother of Jesus, who was not a follower of Jesus in his lifetime but was converted by a resurrection appearance (I Cor 15:7) and then went on to become the leader of the mother church in Jerusalem. This view was eventually accepted by the Church as a whole, though not without considerable hesitation. There are today those who are prepared to defend it, pointing to such features as the letter's tone of authority and strongly Jewish-Christian outlook.

There are serious objections to this view, though. The Greek language and style is much too good to have been written by the Lord's brother whose native tongue was Aramaic. The writer makes no mention of any connection with Jesus and never refers to the Resurrection which must have been all-important to James, the brother of the Lord. Above all, if the work was written by such an outstanding leader of the early Church, why then was this not even suggested until the early fourth century? Why were there so many doubts as to whether it should be in the New Testament at all?

The evidence compels us to admit that we simply do not know who wrote the Letter of James. We can only say that the author was an unknown, Greek-speaking Jewish-Christian.

Do James and Paul Agree?

It is some of the ethical teaching of the letter which has caused problems. The section in 2:14-26 discusses "faith" and "works" and being "justified" — all key terms in the thought of Paul, especially in Galatians and Romans where the fundamentals of the Christian faith as he understands them are discussed. James is obviously combatting what he believes is the *wrong* understanding of faith and works, and the main point he wants to make is that "faith apart from works is dead" (2:17, 2:26). By that he means it is not enough just to believe certain doctrines; our faith must result in actions and in Christian living. We recall the very practical definition of religion which James gives a little earlier: "Religion that is pure and undefiled before God and the Father is this: to visit orphans and widows in their affliction, and to keep oneself unstained from the world" (1:27).

This sounds like both good Christianity and good common sense. The problem arises when we compare what James says here with Paul. When James asks if a person's faith can save him (2:14), he expects his readers to respond with a resounding "No!" In 2:24 he definitely concludes that a person "is justified by works and not by faith alone." But in Rom 3:28 Paul declares that a person "is justified by faith apart from works of law," and in Gal 2:16 he holds that a person "is not justified by the works of the law but through faith in Jesus Christ." (It was on the basis of these texts that Martin Luther made "by faith alone" the great watchword of the Reformation.) Interestingly enough, both Paul and James cite the example of Abraham to support their case. Paul concludes that Abraham was justified by faith (Gal 3:6-9, Rom 4), whereas James asks, "Was not Abraham our father justified by works?" (James 2:21).

Before we jump to the conclusion that there is a hopeless contradiction here, we should note carefully that Paul and James do not mean exactly the same thing by either the term "works" or the term "faith."

Paul's expression is usually "works of law," which really means "legalism." Paul stresses that a person cannot be justified, that is, accepted into a right relationship with God, by piling up the performance of religious rules and rituals. No one can earn or merit God's salvation. Christians are utterly dependent on God's grace received through faith. Of course, when they are in a right relationship with God through faith, their lives are totally transformed and they gladly and willingly obey God and serve others. As we have already seen, justification, in Paul's view, in *by* grace, *through* faith, *for* works.

When James speaks of works he is not thinking of legalistic efforts to win God's favour but of the good deeds which characterize the lives of those who are in a right relationship with God. Paul, therefore, would have no difficulty in agreeing with James here. Of course faith must *result* in works and faith without works is necessarily dead. Paul was as emphatic as anyone that Christian faith must result in Christian living, though he might have preferred to call this "the fruit of the spirit" (Gal 5:22).

When we turn to the term "faith" we find that there is a difference here also. What James means by faith is clear from James 2:19: "You believe that God is one; you do well. Even the demons believe — and shudder." In this view faith or belief means simply intellectual assent. It is "belief *that*" — belief *that* God exists, belief *that* there is only one God. This is a very limited kind of faith. It need not affect the way we live; even the demons believe that there is one God — and much good it does them!

Paul, however, operates with a completely different view of faith. For him, faith means opening up completely to the grace of God. It is through faith that a person enters into a new, living, dynamic relationship with God and receives the gift of the Holy Spirit. It is quite impossible for demons to have *this* kind of faith; if they did, they would become angels! Paul, therefore, would agree with James that mere intellectual assent is not enough, but he would want to argue for a much broader and deeper definition of faith.

Although both Paul and James refer to the example of Abraham, they are thinking of quite different incidents in the life of the patriarch. James (2:21-23) refers to the dramatic story of

Genesis 22 in which Abraham was called upon to sacrifice his only son Isaac. Of course this showed faith, but James emphasizes that Abraham was willing to *act* on his faith; he actually journeyed to the appointed place, built the altar and laid Isaac on it (before the angel of the Lord intervened). Paul, however, is looking back to Genesis 15 where God promises Abraham a son and, through him, many descendants. Abraham's wife Sarah was already in her old age so that what God promised was humanly impossible. Faith in these circumstances means a deep trust that God will transform our lives in a way which we could not possibly accomplish by ourselves. This episode, therefore, is a much better illustration of what Paul means by "faith" — not just a belief *that* certain things are true, but a belief *in* God who can transform our lives.

Our conclusion is that James and Paul do not contradict one another, mainly because most of the time they are not even on the same wavelength. It seems certain that James had never read Paul's letters. The likeliest theory is that he had heard of Paul's views at second or third hand, and that Paul's teaching had reached him only in garbled fashion. Paul's views could be misunderstood or misinterpreted and we must suppose that they had reached James in some such form as, "Works don't matter, all you need is faith." James, then, is not attacking Paul but a misunderstanding or misrepresentation of Paul's teaching.

If Paul had been able to meet James he would certainly have agreed with the main points James makes, but he would probably have felt that James was not a very profound thinker. If James had been able to meet Paul (or read his letters) it is not certain what his reaction would have been. Like many other people he might have found Paul difficult to understand. If and when he eventually grasped the main outlines of Paul's position we can imagine him saying, "Well, if *that* is what you mean by faith and works, then I am in basic agreement with you."

The study of Paul and James is instructive for our understanding of Scripture. We can see how God used and inspired individuals of very different temperaments and outlooks. In God's providence both Paul and James find a place within the New Testament. Paul is by far the more profound and daring thinker and yet, because he can be misunderstood and misrepresented, he needs to be balanced by the practical Christianity of James. The Letter of James itself would be a hopelessly inadequate statement of what Christianity is all about. It very definitely needs to be balanced by the insights of Paul. Christians do not read these writers in isolation; they do not read Paul without James, nor James without Paul. Through both these individuals God's word still challenges believers to accept the offer of God's grace through faith *and* to put their faith into practice in a world which is crying out for help.

19.
The Letters of Peter and Jude

As we can well imagine, it was not easy to be a Christian in New Testament times. Those who became members of the early Church found themselves liable to suspicion, misunderstanding and, often, downright hostility. Relations could be difficult with other members of one's family who were not believers or with an employer or master who was a non-Christian and, especially, with officials of the state who were alarmed at the spread of the new faith and who began to take measures against it. On top of all this the Church had many internal problems which were difficult to resolve.

It is not easy to be a Christian in today's world either. There are many living under Communism in Eastern Europe, the U.S.S.R. and China or under oppressive regimes in Latin America, for example, where the acute pressures they face are not unlike those experienced by the early Christians. Even in Europe and North America believers can no longer assume that they are living in a "Christian country"; rather, we are moving into a "post-Christian" era characterized by growing indifference and sometimes hostility towards those who profess the Christian faith.

The two letters of Peter and that of Jude let us see how the Church coped with such pressures and problems in the early days. Through them God can speak to Christians today and guide them as to how they should live in a non-Christian environment.

Basic Christianity

I Peter is a splendid statement of "basic Christianity." Much of the letter seems to be addressed to recent converts, to those who were formerly in ignorance (1:14), who walked in futile ways (1:18), who were enslaved to human passions (4:2) but who have heard the preaching of the Good News (1:12, 25) and who now believe (2:7). A number of scholars have argued that the main part of the letter (1:3 — 4:11) must have had something to do with the baptismal service by which new converts were admitted into membership of the Church. "Baptism," we read in 3:21, "now saves you..." Those addressed are no longer isolated individuals; having been "born anew" (1:3, 1:23, 2:2), they are like "living stones... built into a spiritual house" (2:5) and are now part of "God's own people" (2:9). It is probably going too far to suggest that in 1:3 — 4:11 we have the wording of a complete baptismal service, but it may be that the letter is partly based on the kind of sermon which the writer was accustomed to giving to new converts at baptism. All members of the congregation would be present at such a service and would hear the sermon, too.

The letter has an opening greeting (1:1, 2) and a closing greeting (5:12-14). Apart from these verses the sermon material seems to run straight on from 1:3 to 4:11, concluding with an ascription of praise. Then there comes a break, and many scholars believe that 4:12 — 5:11 has been added on to the earlier section. The first part of the letter does not seem to reflect any particular crisis in the Church's life. There are references to "various trials" (1:6) and to the possibility of suffering "for righteousness' sake" (3:14), but these are couched in fairly general terms. We have a change, however, at 4:12 which refers to the sudden onset of a "fiery ordeal," and the last section of the letter seems much more directly concerned with suffering "as a Christian" (4:16), for "your adversary the devil is prowling around (present tense) like a roaring lion, seeking someone to devour" (5:8). The suggestion has therefore been made that to the generally worded sermon-type material in 1:3 — 4:11 the author has added some further words of exhortation in 4:12 —

5:11, perhaps just as news came in of the outbreak of persecution.

The letter claims to be by "Peter, an apostle of Jesus Christ" (1:1) and to be written from "Babylon" (5:13) — an early Christian code-word for the city of Rome. The church there sends greetings to the readers and so does Mark (5:13). This fits in well with early traditions that Peter spent his last years in Rome (before being martyred under the Emperor Nero), and that Mark the evangelist was his assistant who later recorded Peter's memories of Jesus. All the early Church writers, who quote the letter, accept it as the work of Simon Peter.

Many are therefore surprised to learn that the authorship of the letter has not gone unchallenged in modern times. For some scholars I Peter is obviously "the work of a man of letters, skilled in all the devices of rhetoric, and able to draw upon an extensive and even learned vocabulary,"[30] whereas, according to Acts 4:13, Peter and John were "uneducated, common men." Moreover, it is held that whereas in the earliest persecutions Christians were arrested for specific crimes, I Peter 4:14 and 4:16 reflect a situation in which simply being a Christian was a crime in itself. The earliest evidence for such a situation relates to the persecution of Christians by Pliny, the governor of Pontus-Bithynia, in Asia Minor, about A.D. 112.

Authorship by Peter has been strongly defended, however, by E. G. Selwyn[31] who points to 5:12 which says that the letter was written "through Silvanus," which is an alternative form of the name, Silas. Now Silas was an important man in the early Church. In Acts 15:22 and 32 he and Judas Barsabbas are described as "leading men among the brethren," and as "prophets"; later, he was a travelling companion and associate of Paul. It could well be, therefore, that while Peter was responsible for the basic content, the letter was written up by Silas who would then be responsible for the good Greek. Further, there is no good reason why chapter 4 should not refer to the persecution under Nero in A.D. 64. A strong argument can thus be made for the traditional view that the letter was written by the apostle Peter. Here again, however, we must remember that the value of the letter and the word it speaks to Christians today does not depend on the question of who actually wrote it.

The Epistle of Hope

The author writes to Christians in several provinces of Asia Minor (1:1) to give them encouragement and hope. Indeed, I Peter is frequently referred to as the "epistle of hope," a commodity often in short supply in our world today. This is no mere whistling in the dark, hoping against hope that things will eventually turn out all right; rather, it is firmly grounded in belief in God by whose great mercy "we have been born anew to a living hope through the resurrection of Jesus Christ from the dead" (1:3).

In difficult times believers have the example of Christ to inspire them: "Christ also suffered for you, leaving you an example, that you should follow in his steps" (2:21). Of course, if Christians merely had this high example they could be completely frustrated trying to follow it. It is therefore important to note that I Peter also gives some of the clearest teaching in the New Testament on the atonement, that is, on how Christ has dealt with both the guilt and power of sin. Christ's death is thought of as a ransom which sets people free (1:18), as replacing the lamb sacrificed at Passover (1:19, cf. Ex 12:5), as the work of the Suffering Servant of Isaiah 53 who bears our sins (2:22-25), and as the sprinkled blood which seals the new covenant (1:2, cf. Ex 24:7, 8).

Those who have been ransomed from their former futile ways are called to live new and different lives. They are to be "holy" (1:15, 16), the basic meaning of which is "separate" or "different" and, hence, "set apart for God's service." New converts suffer abuse from their former companions because they no longer participate in their drinking parties and licentious life style (4:3, 4). With Christians it is definitely not a case of "when in Rome, do as the Romans do." How far, one wonders, can Church members today claim to be "different," by sharing in a distinctive and easily recognizable life style?

Christians are to silence criticism by showing a good example in all their dealings with others (2:11, 12). They are to be good citizens and pray for their rulers even when these are not Christians (2:13-17). Slaves are to be obedient to their masters even if they are unjustly treated (2:18-25). Obviously, at this early stage, when Christians were such a tiny minority, there was no question of trying to change the structure of society or of effecting reforms. This became possible for Christians only in later centuries. Mutual obligations for wives and husbands are spelled out (3:1-7). The advice to wives is particularly interesting since it seems to assume that the husbands are non-Christians; in such cases the wives are advised to use a form of "silent evangelism," seeking to win their partners for the faith, not by anything they say, but by the sheer quality of their Christian living.

Some Christians are good at expressing themselves; they are the kind of people who must "always be prepared to make a defence" of their faith (3:15). Others can witness most effectively by the lives they live. Whatever gifts God has bestowed, they should be used for others: "whoever speaks, as one who utters oracles of God; whoever renders service, as one who renders it by the strength which God supplies" (4:11).

The Gnostic Challenge

Jude and II Peter are among the shortest and, almost certainly, the latest books of the New Testament. There is some connection between them because 19 of Jude's 25 verses also appear in II Peter. Most scholars hold that Jude was written first and that the writer of II Peter borrowed extensively from it in writing his second chapter.

The background of Jude is a serious crisis in the life of the Church: the Christian congregation concerned was being infiltrated by "ungodly persons" who were perverting the truth of the Gospel and causing scandal in the Church by the way they behaved. Although very little is said regarding their beliefs, they almost certainly represented a form of Gnosticism, that movement which as we have already noted claimed a special *gnōsis* or "knowledge" and which was such a threat to the Church, especially in the second century. These people "set up divisions" (verse 19), regarding themselves as a superior grade of Christians to whom the ordinary rules of morality do not apply. When the Church members meet for their "love feasts" (common meals which included the celebration of the Lord's Supper) these people "boldly carouse together" (verse 12).

Jude does not so much argue with the offenders as denounce them. He sounds like a preacher who produces a whole string of illustrations to get his point across: three from the Old Testament in verses 5-7 and another three in verse 11, quotations from a couple of apocryphal books (*The Assumption of Moses* in verse 9, and the *Book of Enoch* in verses 14, 15) and some quite flowery rhetoric when he denounces the ungodly as "waterless clouds," "fruitless trees," "wild waves" and "wandering stars" (verses 12, 13). Jude warns his readers — and Christians today — that believers can never afford to rest on their oars. They must always be alert for those, even within the Church, who will betray the Gospel by word and deed and they must be ready "to contend for the faith which was once for all delivered to the saints" (verse 3).

Jude (or Judas) was a common name. Since he introduces himself as the brother of James (verse 1), it has been supposed that he is the Jude listed as a brother of Jesus (see Mark 6:3). Yet since the letter seems to look back from a distance to the time of the apostles (verse 17), he was probably a Church leader of the late first or even early second century. The question has been raised as to whether Jude even deserves a place in the New Testament. Yet, one can easily see that his warnings could apply in any age, and he does close with a beautiful benediction which was probably already in use in the worship services of the Church of his day (vs. 24, 25).

II Peter seems to be written to people who have been Christians for some time. They are "established in the truth" (1:12), though the writer feels that there are certain basic Christian principles of which they need to be reminded. They evidently faced much the same kind of situation as lies behind the letter of Jude, and this writer, in chapter 2, borrows quite extensively from Jude in denouncing the false teachers who are causing all the trouble.

The authorship of II Peter raises difficult problems. On the one hand the letter claims to be written by the apostle Peter (1:1), refers to his part in the Transfiguration story (1:17, 18) and refers back to I Peter (3:1). On the other hand, there are clear indications that it was written long after the early days of the Church (3:4); it borrows extensively from Jude which is a late work and it shows a knowledge of much of the New Testament (Paul's letters, which are regarded as Scripture — 3:15, 16; at least one of the first three Gospels — 1:17; John's

Gospel — 1:13, 14; I Peter — 3:1; and, of course, Jude). This indicates a date long after Peter's time and on into the second century. Even many conservative scholars admit that the letter may not have been written by Peter. This is not exactly "modernism" since the letter was doubted by many of the early Church fathers and, at the time of the Reformation, John Calvin was among those who held that the letter could not have been written by Peter. We must suppose, then, that some second century Church leader wrote in Peter's name to combat the dangers which were threatening the Church.

God's Time-Scale Not Ours

II Peter 3 deals with another pressing problem that has also worried believers in other times. Some Christians in the early Church expected the second coming of Christ to occur soon, certainly in their own lifetime. As time went on and one generation succeeded another without any sign of the end, Christians found themselves being mocked and scoffed at by people who asked sarcastically, "Where is the promise of his coming?" (3:4). The author provides his readers with a series of arguments to refute those who scoff in this way (3:5-10), reminding them that God's time-scale is not the same as ours and reaffirming the position found elsewhere in the New Testament — not that the end will come *soon* but, rather, that it will come *suddenly* and *unexpectedly*. History only makes sense if it has a final goal: in the midst of a world of sin and suffering believers can be sustained by the assurance that, ultimately, evil will be defeated and God will usher in a new order consisting of "new heavens and a new earth in which righteousness dwells" (3:13).

The Christian Apocalypse

20. The Book of Revelation

The Book of Revelation has caused Christian believers more problems than any other work in the New Testament. It has been the happy hunting ground of religious cranks who use it to explain to you in great detail (if you let them get their foot in your front door) exactly how and when the world is going to come to an end. In the early centuries it was the last book accepted into the New Testament. At the time of the Reformation Martin Luther seems to have doubted whether it should be part of the Christian Scriptures; he felt that, in Revelation, Christ is "neither taught nor recognized."[32] It is a book which makes almost no reference to the earthly life of Jesus, has little to say on such Christian virtues as humility, love and forgiveness, makes a rigid distinction between the righteous and the wicked, but seems to have little or no interest in redeeming the wicked. Yet it cannot simply be handed over for the sects to exploit. It is part of the New Testament and, while it deals with only some aspects of the Christian faith, it has much more significance and relevance for the twentieth century than most Christians realize.

Apart from the first chapter which serves as an introduction, the book clearly falls into two parts: in chapters 2 and 3 we have the Letters to the Seven Churches, while in chapters 4 to 22 we have the Revelation (or Apocalypse) proper.

Shaking the Comfortable Pew

The Letters are not too difficult to understand. They were written to Christian congregations in the Roman province of Asia (the western part of modern Turkey), at Ephesus, Smyrna, Pergamum, Thyatira, Sardis, Philadelphia and Laodicea. Each letter follows a standard format but the varying mixture of praise and blame shows that the writer is well acquainted with what is happening in each individual congregation. It is possible that a messenger travelled round the seven churches delivering the letters as he went and that they were later copied and collected.

The main problem in reading the letters is that we know so little about these cities and about the groups of Christians who are being addressed. In modern times, however, historical research and archaeological discoveries have shed a flood of light on the letters. For example, the letter to Laodicea (3:14-22) really comes alive when we know that Laodicea was a rich, proud city which, after an earthquake in A.D. 60, actually scorned federal government assistance and rebuilt itself entirely from its own resources. The city was noted for its wealth, for it was a great centre of trade and banking; it was noted for its clothing industry, based on a highly prized, dark, soft, glossy wool produced in the area; and it had a famous medical school with a related drug industry which produced a special type of powder for treating eye diseases. Evidently, the church at Laodicea mirrored the pride and self-sufficiency of the community in which it was situated; it said, "I am rich, I have prospered, and I need nothing." Obviously, the writer has the local background very much in mind when he tells the Laodicean church members sharply that they are in fact "poor, blind and naked." He counsels them to buy "*gold* refined by fire"; they imagine that they are rich, but they are poor in the things that really count. He tells them to buy "*white garments* to clothe you"; rather than their expensive black coats, they need to wear the pure white robes of the saints. He advises them to purchase "*salve* to anoint your eyes"; they have to come to see themselves as they really are. A knowledge of the local references thus opens up the message of the letter, a message which is surely just as relevant today when the Church exists in an affluent society and in a world where so many think they have no need of God.

When we study these letters (preferably with the help of a good commentary)[33] we discover that each congregation had a character of its own, and that several of them bear an extraordinarily life-like resemblance to congregations of the present day! The church at Laodicea doubtless had a healthy bank balance but it is condemned for its complacency: "Because you are *lukewarm,* and neither cold nor hot, I will spew you out of my mouth." This is the kind of word Christians need today to shake them out of the comfortable pews in which they are so often content to sit.

Symbolism and Code

Chapters 4 to 22 are written in a style and format which seem very strange, if not quite incomprehensible, to most people today. We have to realize that it would not be strange to the first readers of Revelation. The "apocalypse" was a popular type of book, especially in the period between the Old and New Testaments. Many such Jewish works are known to us, one example being *The War of the Sons of Light with the Sons of Darkness* which was discovered among the Dead Sea Scrolls.

The New Testament Book of Revelation is the Christian apocalypse; it uses the apocalypse format (though with some changes). There are two features of an apocalypse which we must recognize straight away. The first is its use of *imagery* and *symbolism.* When the author speaks of the coming reign of God he is really seeking to describe the indescribable. Jaspar walls, golden streets and pearly gates are not to be taken literally; the most beautiful and precious things known here on earth are used as symbols or signposts pointing towards a reality which eye has not seen nor heart conceived. In order to understand the vision of the Holy City in Revelation 21, we are likely to get much more help from an artist or a poet than from a surveyor. The second feature of an apocalypse is its use of a *secret code.* These books were usually written in times of persecution. If they fell into the hands of the enemy the code ensured that they appeared to be meaningless and thus harmless. Believers who knew the code, however, could understand exactly what was being said. Thus it would be dangerous to write a book prophesying the downfall of Rome, the power which was persecuting the Christian Church. So Revelation says, "Babylon the great city shall be thrown down" (18:21). If you are on the same wavelength as the writer, then you know that "Babylon" is actually the codeword for "Rome."

Fortunately, modern scholars have been able to decipher the symbolism and the code of Revelation to a considerable extent. As a result, a further point is abundantly clear. The book did not try to reveal what will happen in the 1980s or 1990s (what could be more irrelevant to a little group of persecuted Asian Christians in A.D. 95?), nor did it provide a crystal ball prediction of the history of the next twenty centuries. The book is to be understood in the first instance in terms of the period in which it was written.

In the reign of the Emperor Domitian, around A.D. 95, the Church in Asia evidently found itself on a collision course with the state on the question of Emperor worship. For Rome this was really a test of political loyalty; once you had made a token offering of incense to the Emperor you could go back home and follow your own religion. Domitian claimed to be "Dominus et Deus" — Lord and God — a claim no Christian could accept. The Church faced a form of *totalitarianism* where the state (in the person of the Emperor) claimed a person's total and ultimate loyalty. Christians sought to be good citizens but they believed that their ultimate loyalty must be to God alone. They were prepared to pray *for* the Emperor but not *to* the Emperor. Thus, the Church found itself subject to a fierce persecution. Totalitarianism has not been confined to the first century: our own century has seen too many examples of dictatorship, of the worship of the state and of the terrible results which flow from such misplaced loyalty.

Jewish apocalypses were generally ascribed to a figure in the distant past, but the author of Revelation identifies himself by name simply as "John" (1:1, 4, 9). He was, he tells us, "on the island called Patmos on account of the word of God and the testimony of Jesus." John evidently had been exiled to this lonely spot in the Aegean Sea because of his Christian profession. To the seven churches on the mainland he was obviously a person of considerable authority. Later tradition identified him with the apostle John, though it is not certain whether or not this is correct. When he speaks of "the twelve names of the twelve apostles of the lamb" (21:14) on the foundations of the Holy City, it certainly sounds more like someone who is not himself one of the twelve looking back with reverence on the founders of the Church. The author claims only that his book is a "prophecy" (1:3; 22:7, 10, 18, 19). The fact is that we cannot identify the author with certainty.

The Throne of God

John's message was directed in the first instance to the seven churches of Asia. Yet, once we have grasped what he was saying to these early Christians, we can hear him speaking to our own day also. Revelation presents us with a tremendous vision of God as the ruler of all of human history. Again and again the author returns to the symbol of "the throne of God." It may not be too difficult for many Christians today to say that they believe in "the sovereignty of God"; however, for John, living in a situation in which sinister forces of evil seemed to be everywhere triumphant and in which it looked as though the Christian Church would be crushed out of existence, it was a tremendous act of faith to assert that God is still on the throne.

Revelation also teaches (despite Luther) that God is supremely revealed in Jesus Christ. In the circumstances we should not be surprised that attention is focussed most of the time on the risen, triumphant and exalted Christ. (Here, of course, Revelation needs to be supplemented and balanced by the reading of the Gospels.) Christ is portrayed as the conquering "*Lion* of the tribe of Judah" (5:5), but also as "the *Lamb* who was slain" (5:12). John shows us a Christ who did not conquer by force of arms but by his own self-sacrifice on the Cross and by shedding his blood to "ransom people for God from every tribe and tongue and people and nation" (5:9).

The Powers of Evil

John constantly reminds us that evil is a real and powerful force in history. God rules, but in the present age he is opposed by Satan and the powers of evil. With keen insight John sees how a system like the Roman Empire, when it goes beyond its God-given limits, can become demonic, that is, controlled by the powers of evil, and how an individual can become a personification of these powers. Such a view was very unpalatable to the liberal optimism dominant in Victorian times and in the early part of this century which was so confident that our civilization was on an escalator, steadily progressing upwards, and that with universal education and the spread of science the world was bound to get better and better. A century which has seen two world wars, the Holocaust, the atom bomb and endless examples of inhumanity may now be readier to concede that John's analysis of the human condition is not so much pessimistic as realistic.

The reference in chapter 20 to the thousand year reign of Christ (the Millennium) has aroused endless controversy. Perhaps it suggests limited progress within history. There can be periods (the 1000 years is surely not to be taken literally) when the Gospel will spread, when the martyrs will be vindicated, when both individuals and societies will be won for Christ. At the same time, we must never forget what comes immediately after the millennium: "When the thousand years are ended, Satan will be loosed from his prison" (20:7). Here we have a vivid symbol of the persistence of the powers of evil. Christians can never afford to coast. Just when we think we have made progress in one area, evil is liable to pop up again in another, in a new and terrible form. History, therefore, is a constant struggle between the forces of good and evil, a struggle in which believers are summoned to participate. Of course, the final victory will be God's (20:7-22:5), but this lies beyond history rather than within history as we know it.

The Role of the Church

Revelation reminds us that the Church has a leading part in God's purposes. John does not call the Christian community to be successful but to be faithful. The prime task of Christians is to witness to their faith in whatever situation God has placed them and at whatever cost may be involved. In 2:13, Antipas, a member of the congregation at Pergamum, is called, "my witness, my faithful one"; the Greek word for witness is *martys* from which we get our word "martyr." The context shows that Antipas was one of those who was faithful even unto death. How can a Church endure such a time of trial and testing? Part of the answer lies in the emphasis on worship which pervades the book. During Sunday worship John hears the risen Christ speaking (1:10). The heavenly hosts are repeatedly portrayed as praising God. The Church on earth is linked with the Church in heaven. The two can join together in one great song of praise: "Hallelujah! For the Lord our God the Almighty reigns. Let us rejoice and exult and give him the glory" (19:6, 7).

Here is a book which offers no easy optimism or superficial faith but, rather, a profound Christian interpretation of the problems of sin and suffering. In a day and age when many can only survey the future with pessimism and despair, it challenges Christians to a more faithful witness and assures them that "the sovereignty of the world has passed to our Lord and his Christ, and he shall reign for ever and ever!" (11:15 *New English Bible*).

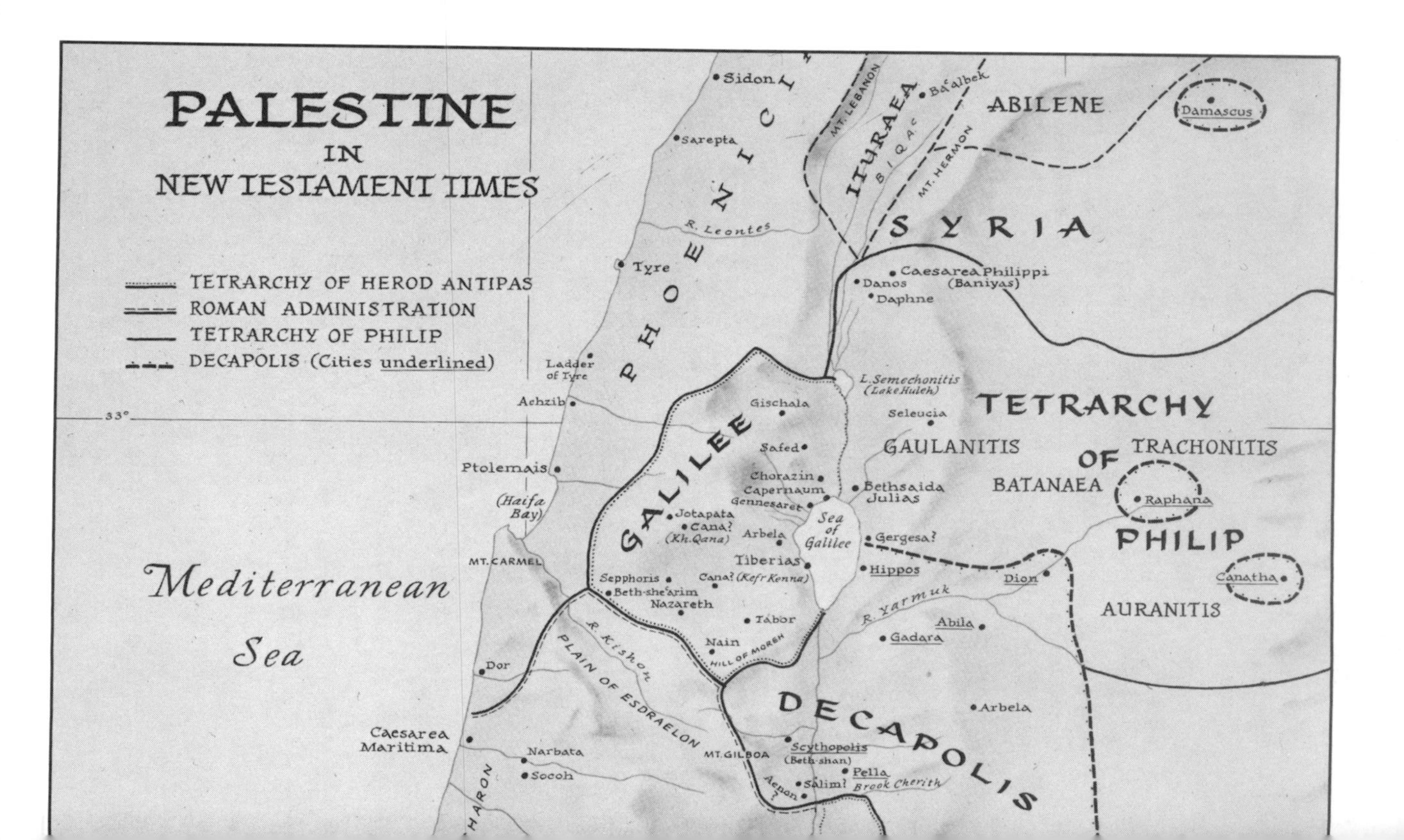

PALESTINE
IN
NEW TESTAMENT TIMES
TETRARCHY OF HEROD ANTIPAS
ROMAN ADMINISTRATION
TETRARCHY OF PHILIP
DECAPOLIS (Cities underlined)
33°
Mediterranean
Sea
PHOENICIA
SYRIA
ABILENE
ITURAEA
TETRARCHY OF PHILIP
TRACHONITIS
GAULANITIS
BATANAEA
AURANITIS
GALILEE
DECAPOLIS
Damascus
Canatha
Raphana
Dion
Abila
Arbela
Gadara
Hippos
Gergesa?
Pella
Scythopolis
(Beth-shan)
Brook Cherith
Salim?
Aenon?
Sidon
Sarepta
R. Leontes
Tyre
Ladder of Tyre
Achzib
Ptolemais
(Haifa Bay)
MT. CARMEL
Dor
Caesarea Maritima
Narbata
Socoh
SHARON
PLAIN OF ESDRAELON
R. Kishon
MT. GILBOA
HILL OF MOREH
Nain
Tabor
Nazareth
Beth-she'arim
Sepphoris
Cana?
Jotapata
Cana?
(Kh. Qana)
(Kefr Kenna)
Tiberias
Arbela
Gennesaret
Capernaum
Chorazin
Safed
Gischala
Sea of Galilee
Bethsaida Julias
Seleucia
L. Semechonitis
(Lake Huleh)
Danos
Daphne
Caesarea Philippi
(Baniyas)
MT. HERMON
MT. LEBANON
BIQA'
Ba'albek
R. Yarmuk

PEREA
NABATEA
JUDEA
IDUMEA
Dead Sea
(Lake Asphaltitis)
Philadelphia
(Rabbah)
Araq el-Emir
Medeba
Machaerus
Callirrhoe
R. Arnon
R. Jabbok
R. Jordan
Gadara
Brook of Zered
Petra
0
10
20
30
miles
(Nablus)
Sychar?
MT. GERIZIM
Salim?
Apollonia
Sozusa
Capharsaba
Brook of Kanah
Pharaton
Coreae
Alexandrium
Antipatris?
Joppa
Rathamin
(Arimathea?)
Shiloh
Phasaelis
Ephraim
Aphairema
Lydda
Adida
Modein
Bethel
Archelais
Sappho
Lower Beth-horon
Upper Beth-horon
Michmash
Dok
Jabneh
(Jamnia)
Gazara
Gabaon
Capharsalama
Taurus
Jericho
Cyprus
Kedron
Emmaus?
(Nicopolis)
Cariathiareim
Emmaus?
(Qubeibeh)
Jerusalem
Bethphage
Bethany
Ekron
Azotus
Qumran
Hyrcania
Bethlehem
Bethbasi
Beth-zechariah
Etam
Herodium
Ascalon
Beth-zaith
Thekoa
Capharabis
WILDERNESS OF JUDEA
Beth-zur
Hebron
Gaza
En-gedi
Masada
Raphia
Beer-sheba
32°
31°
35°
36°

THE WORLD OF THE NEW TESTAMENT

ROME AND THE EASTERN MEDITERRANEAN

Boundary of the Roman Empire — Provincial boundaries — + Seven Churches of Asia

0 100 200 300 400 500 miles

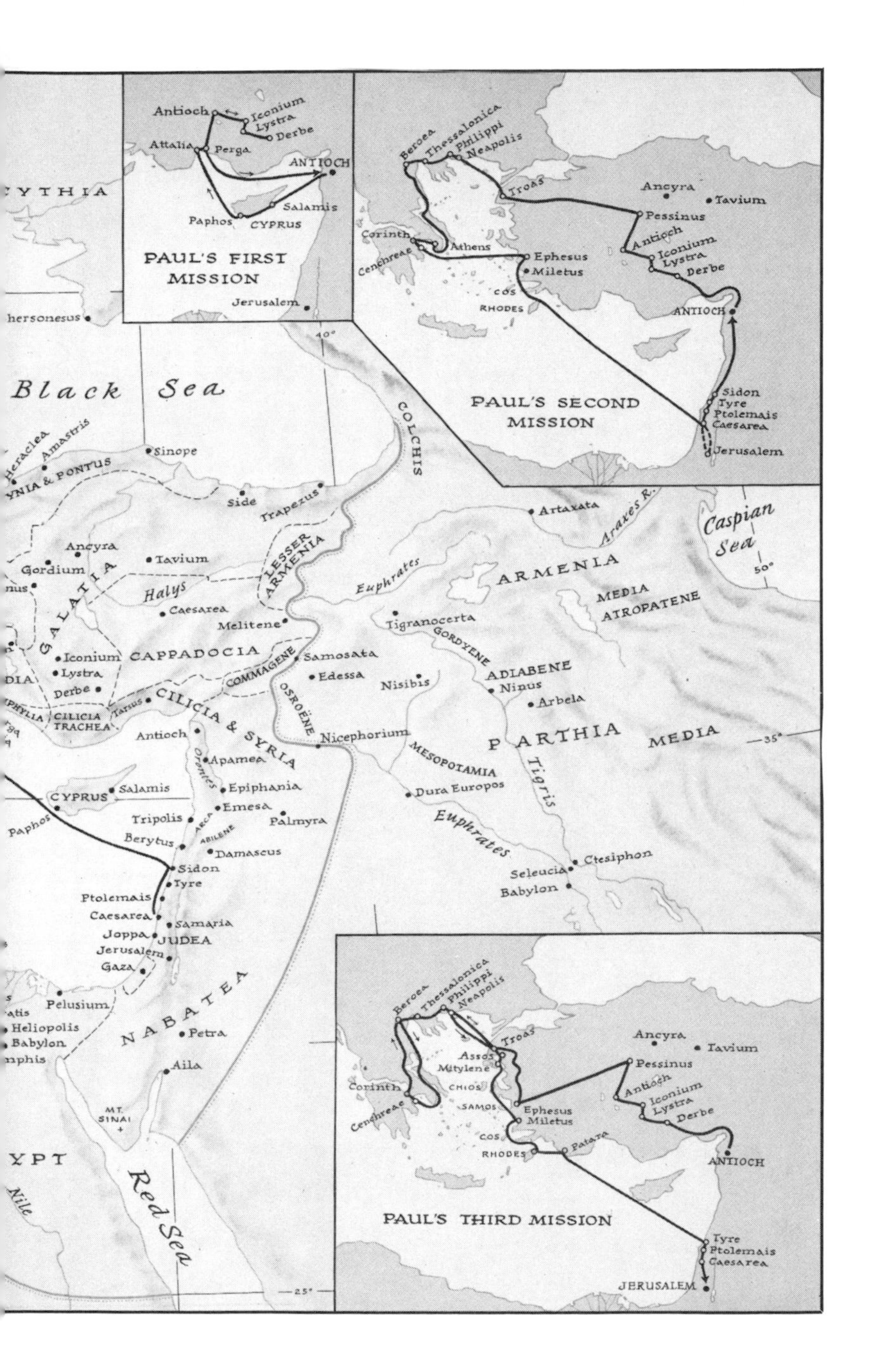
PAUL'S FIRST MISSION
Antioch
Iconium
Lystra
Derbe
Attalia
Perga
ANTIOCH
Paphos
CYPRUS
Salamis
Jerusalem
PAUL'S SECOND MISSION
Beroea
Thessalonica
Philippi
Neapolis
Troas
Ancyra
Tavium
Pessinus
Antioch
Iconium
Lystra
Derbe
Corinth
Cenchreae
Athens
Ephesus
Miletus
COS
RHODES
ANTIOCH
Sidon
Tyre
Ptolemais
Caesarea
Jerusalem
PAUL'S THIRD MISSION
Assos
Mitylene
CHIOS
SAMOS
Patara
JERUSALEM
Black Sea
Caspian Sea
COLCHIS
Sinope
Heraclea
Amastris
PONTUS
Side
Trapezus
Artaxata
Araxes R.
LESSER ARMENIA
ARMENIA
Euphrates
Tavium
Gordium
GALATIA
Halys
Caesarea
Melitene
MEDIA ATROPATENE
Tigranocerta
GORDYENE
CAPPADOCIA
COMMAGENE
Samosata
Edessa
Nisibis
ADIABENE
Ninus
Arbela
CILICIA TRACHEA
Tarsus
CILICIA & SYRIA
OSROËNE
Nicephorium
MESOPOTAMIA
PARTHIA
MEDIA
Tigris
Orontes
Apamea
Epiphania
Emesa
Palmyra
Tripolis
Berytus
ABILENE
Damascus
Dura Europos
Ctesiphon
Seleucia
Babylon
Sidon
Tyre
Ptolemais
Caesarea
Samaria
Joppa
JUDEA
Jerusalem
Gaza
NABATEA
Petra
Aila
Pelusium
Heliopolis
Babylon
MT. SINAI
Red Sea
Nile
40°
50°
35°
25°

Footnotes

1. See H. C. Kee, *Jesus in History: An Approach to the Study of the Gospels* (New York: Harcourt, Brace & World, 1970), chapter 2, "Jesus in Extrabiblical Sources," pp. 29-61.
2. A. Schweitzer, *The Quest of the Historical Jesus* (New York: Macmillan, 1910. Third edition, with new introduction, 1954).
3. Irenaeus, *Against Heresies,* III, 11.
4. Tacitus, *Annals,* XV, 44.
5. Pliny the Younger, *Letters,* X, 96.
6. See M. Staniforth, *Early Christian Writings: The Apostolic Fathers* (Harmondsworth: Penguin, 1968).
7. See M. R. James, *The Apocryphal New Testament* (Oxford: Clarendon Press, 1924); E. Hennecke, W. Schneemelcher, R. McL. Wilson, *New Testament Apocrypha,* 2 vols. (Philadelphia: Westminster, 1963, 1964).
8. See J. M. Robinson, *The Nag Hammadi Library in English* (New York: Harper and Row, 1977).
9. D. Daube, "Jesus and the Samaritan Woman: The Meaning of σuyXpαoμαi," *Journal of Biblical Literature,* 69 (1950), pp. 137-147.
10. See E. P. Sanders, *Paul and Palestinian Judaism* (Philadelphia: Fortress Press, 1977).
11. M. Barth, *The Broken Wall: A Study of the Epistle to the Ephesians* (Valley Forge: Judson Press, 1959).
12. E. J. Goodspeed, *The Meaning of Ephesians: A Study of the Origin of the Epistle* (Chicago: University Press, 1933).
13. Quoted in Eusebius, *Ecclesiastical History,* III, 39.
14. Irenaeus, *Against Heresies,* III, 1:2.
15. See V. Corbo, *The House of St. Peter at Capharnaum* (Jerusalem: Franciscan Press, 1969).

16. N. Perrin, D. C. Duling, *The New Testament: An Introduction,* 2nd. edition, (New York: Harcourt Brace Jovanovich, 1982) p. 238.
17. Quoted in Eusebius, *Ecclesiastical History,* III, 39.
18. Irenaeus, *Against Heresies,* III, 1:1; *Muratonian Canon.*
19. H. Conzelmann, *The Theology of St. Luke* (London: Faber and Faber, 1960).
20. See W. W. Gasque, *A History of the Criticism of the Acts of the Apostles* (Grand Rapids: Eerdmans, 1975), p. 122.
21. Clement of Alexandria, quoted in Eusebius, *Ecclesiastical History,* VI, 14:7.
22. Quoted in Eusebius, *Ecclesiastical History,* III, 39:3f.
23. C. H. Dodd, *The Johannine Epistles,* The Moffatt New Testament Commentary (London: Hodder and Stoughton, 1946), pp. xlvii-lvi.
24. Irenaeus, *Against Heresies,* I, 26:1.
25. R. Law, *The Tests of Life: A study of the First Epistle of St. John* (Edinburgh: Clark, 1909 — 3rd. Edition, 1914).
26. Origen, quoted in Eusebius, *Ecclesiastical History,* VI, 25:11-14.
27. E. Kasemann, *The Wandering People of God: An Investigation of the Letter to the Hebrews* (Minneapolis: Augsburg, 1984). Translated from the German second edition of 1957 (first edition, 1938).
28. M. Luther, "Preface to the New Testament," 1522; English translation in J. Pelican, H. T. Lehmann, editors, *Luther's Works* (Philadelphia: Fortress, 1955 onwards), Vol. 35, p. 362.
29. Eusebius, *Ecclesiastical History,* II, 23.
30. F. W. Beare, *The First Epistle of Peter* (Oxford: Blackwell, 1947 — 3rd. Edition, 1970), pp. 46, 47.
31. E. G. Selwyn, *The First Epistle of St. Peter* (London: Macmillan, 1946 — 2nd. Edition, 1947).
32. M. Luther, "Preface to the Book of Revelation," 1522.
33. See W. Barclay, *Letters to the Seven Churches* (New York: Abingdon, 1957).

Index